Architectural Body

Architectural Body

Madeline Gins and Arakawa

THE UNIVERSITY OF ALABAMA PRESS
Tuscaloosa

Copyright © 2002
The University of Alabama Press
Tuscaloosa, Alabama 35487-0380
All rights reserved
Manufactured in the United States of America

Typeface: AGaramond and Syntax

∞
The paper on which this book is printed meets the minimum requirements of American National Standard for Information Science–Permanence of Paper for Printed Library Materials, ANSI Z39.48–1984.

Library of Congress Cataloging-in-Publication Data

Gins, Madeline.
   Architectural body / Madeline Gins and Arakawa.
      p.   cm. — (Modern and contemporary poetics)
Includes index.
   ISBN 0-8173-1168-8 (cloth : alk. paper) — ISBN 0-8173-1169-6
(pbk. : alk. paper)
   1. Architecture—Philosophy. I. Arakawa, Shûsaku, 1936– II. Title. III. Series.
   NA2500 .G455 2002
   720'.1—dc21

                                                                2002001061

British Library Cataloguing-in-Publication Data available

Dedication

To those who have wanted to go on
living and been unable to

and therefore
even more so

To transhumans

Contents

Preface

"After all this back-and-forth about the title for this book, have we ended up with the right one?"

"If only readers could come to it having some sense of what an architectural body is."

"What was our last other choice for a title?"

"Constructing Life."

"We couldn't take it as the title because our work has more to do with recasting or reconfiguring life than with an out-and-out constructing of it."

"We wanted it because it signaled the connection between what we do and work being done in the fields of self-organization, autopoiesis, artificial life, and consciousness studies."

"The direction is the same. We're on the same avenue. Even so, we're doing something quite different."

"Should we spell out the differences?"

"Not this time around."

New York, 2002

Introduction

Having observed near and far how the body moves through its surroundings, having thought lengthily of still other ways to surround it, and having built a few tactically posed surroundings, we now notice ourselves to have been tracing an architectural body, or at least a landscape for one. We see architecture not merely as that which stands by and gets linked up with, as structures that life lightly avails itself of in passing; not passive, not passively merely hanging around to provide shelter or monumentality, architecture as we newly conceive it actively participates in life and death matters.

Architecture, in anyone's definition of it, exists primarily to be at the service of the body. The question arises as to how to be most fully at the service of the body. Who would not want to live in a world built to serve the body to the nth degree? The question arises as to what the body is in the first place. Serving the body to the nth degree will include as much as the body bargains for and more. It is mandated for the body that it fend off its own demise, and an architecture that would be unstinting toward the body, that would slavishly deliver up to the body all that it would seem to need, must take this as its mandate too.

Once people realize that the human race has not yet availed itself of its greatest tool for learning how not to die, they will cease being defeatists in the matter. Although our species, like every other species, has a characteristic architecture that serves its members well by increasing their chances of survival, it is far from having an architecture that could redefine life. The architecture we speak of in this book is within our species' reach. It will be a way to undo, loosening to widen and re-cast, the concept of person. People will not be defeatists about a condition—the human condition—about which something can be done. The procedural architecture outlined in the pages that follow will function both as spur to and mainstay of an all-out effort to alter the untenable human lot.

Who or what are we as this species? Puzzle creatures to ourselves, we are visitations of inexplicability. What is in fact the case? We must surely go to all possible lengths to find out what we exist in regard to. I want to find out, and so do I, what indeed is the case for those who sniff around this planet as us. We, the members of this species, have thus far failed to come up with a set of explanatory statements that could be universally countenanced as the definitive figuring out of ourselves.

To figure ourselves out, to find out the operative basis of what moves as us and what we find fit to accord value to, we need to learn what makes the world tick. But whenever someone attempts to break open the world to see what makes it tick, to find operative hidden treasures, the world closes ranks as more world and that's it. Figuring ourselves out must include determining what coheres as sentience. But sentience would seem constitutionally unable to determine either how it came about or what coheres as it; sentience always delivers more sentience as world. What are the particles and what are the waves of sentience? We cannot get beyond the world to find out what operates as it, because it is of our making; it is us. And if, because we can never distance ourselves enough from ourselves to assess the whole in its particulars, because the world always gets in our way as still more world, should we not, then, judge as correct Wittgenstein's assertion that "The value of the world must lie outside of the world"? The world, all that comes our way as world, is contingent on we know not what, on what try as we might to get at we never can; breaking through to the we know not what upon which the lived-world is contingent so that we may know its operative basis would seem impossible.

But Wittgenstein's assertion lacks the most important of axiological anchors. It is vague in regard to the assigner of values: For precisely whom must the value of the world lie outside the world? Those being led to contemplate an estranged value are most likely the only ones considering it. If we read the assertion as referring, up to and through some godlike entity in a godless era, to the human subject as assigner of value, it must be seen as committing the error of shutting out peremptorily the issue of our being puzzle creatures to ourselves. The asserter also doesn't take into consideration either the way our own existences are contingent on, take shape in respect to, the actions we take, or the way we comply with the universe to make the world. Perhaps it is not only impossible but also insufficient and unnecessary to approach finding out what the upshot of the world is, its ultimate value, through trying to get beyond or beneath the world. Perhaps the answers rest in, and will be forthcoming from, how the world rushes in as more world to cover the world, a complexity of within rather than one of beyond. Our species has thus far been at a loss as to how to make this work to good effect for the figuring out of itself, and the world, in its pulsing contingency, drowns us, as an ancient-modern poet put it to us. But an incredibly wonderful thing about the contingent is that it can be handled, and reconsidered, and reworked. Instead of trying to have it both ways at once, which is how Wittgenstein inadvertently tried it (the axiological judge that is elsewhere judges for us and through us), why not keep the axiological action right up close? Let the assigner of value pursue her own contingency to the point that it rains down value on her. For those who have no choice but to be contingent, the engineering of contingency is all that is the case: "The value (read *upshot*) of the world must lie in (the complex managing of) its contingency." This book deals with contingency in all its vivacity, with a linking and re-linking of the body and the world to one another—not that the two have ever been apart. Through a newly conceived architecture, the world gets invited in to be a different world. Rearrangements of the world should be able to cause the value (read *upshot*) of the world to become apparent right here in the midst of things.

What, if anything, can constitute the figuring out of ourselves? We contend that philosophical puzzles cannot be solved short of a thorough architectural reworking. It is necessary to track how a world comes to be organized in the vicinity of the human organism. Questions need to be asked in a three-hundred-and-sixty-degree way. Context is all, and all contexts lead to the architectural context, newly conceived. Surroundings can pose questions by virtue of how their elements and features are posed. All that follows here will prove this to be no mere play on words. Depending on what activates what in question-posing surroundings, or on what stimulates bodies to move through these surroundings, answers will tentatively surface, or further questions will.

Without doubt, the human race has hideously acquiesced in regard to its own abysmal fate. Underlying all cultures, in East and West alike, is this assumption or attitudinal stance: we—each and every one of us—must die, no doubt about it, for all those who lived before us died. So unquestionably mortal are we that we have even come to call ourselves mortals, for God's sake. Everyone everywhere wants to insist on this. A bunch of defeatists all. Nobody wants to be caught not getting the "real" straight, for not accurately registering what comes to pass puts one at odds with society. How could what so evidently stares one in the face not be, after all, what it rings true as? We contend that the whole crowd has it all wrong.

Questions about the nature and purpose of our species cannot be answered through reflection alone. Questions and answers are always handled body-wide, whether or not this is recognized to be part of the questioning process at the moment of questioning. Depending on reflection alone represents too drastic a reduction, one that unnecessarily distorts the picture, when it is the body that is being queried as to itself. How does the human body—together with its environment—accomplish what it manages to? How is it possible that she who is a body walks and talks? How much does the body avail itself of its environment when, in the course of behaving in all respects as if it were a person, it serves up thoughtful behavior or comes up with an idea? The body can yield answers through that which it subsists as, through the whole of itself, inclusive of its sequences of actions and the surroundings into which, in a variety of ways, it extends itself. The investigative work that can yield answers cannot be done in the abstract; it must, on the contrary, be done on-site where living happens. Only subsequent to there having been an architectural revolution, a thorough re-visioning of architecture, will difficult questions such as those above call forth answers in the bodies of our contemporaries.

That mortality has been the prevailing condition throughout the ages does not mean it will always have to be. Any resistance mounted thus far against mortality, that ineluctable asphyxiator, has been conducted in too piecemeal a fashion. How can human beings rid themselves of the defeatist attitude that leads them to accept unquestioningly their own inevitable obliteration? Be unrelenting when faced with the relentless. The effort to counter mortality must be constant, persistent, and total. The wish and will to do this must be in the air we breathe, having been built into the places within which we live and breathe. Architecture must be made to fit the body as a second, third, fourth, and, when necessary, ninth (and counting) skin. We believe that people closely and complexly allied with their architectural surrounds can succeed in outliving their (seemingly inevitable) death sentences!

There continues to be something fundamentally wrong with the way our species approaches the puzzle of itself. Generation after generation, our species, not trying all that it could on its own behalf, has made nice with its glaring vulnerability. At best, we move in a morass of inconclusive investigations and fragmentary pursuits; at worst, it is assumed that our species will always remain a mystery to itself. It has of course by now been ascertained that the more a person learns about herself as a functioning organism, and the more she takes cognizance of what she learns in this regard, incorporating it into her routine, the less likely will she be to harm herself. We therefore ought to take pains not to limit ourselves in any way in this respect. It must never be forgotten that we don't know what we are in the first place.

Although the human condition is a crisis condition if ever there was one, few individuals and societies act with the dispatch a state of emergency requires. The fact that the human condition is a crisis condition gets routinely covered up, with culture invariably functioning to obscure how dire the condition is and to float it as bearable. The crisis—that we live in a state of crisis: that all goes down the drain, all—has been put on permanent hold, and the species, oblivious to its own desperateness, goes off on tangents.

Much of the liveliness on this planet registers numb. In the numb register—so much of this that we find around us. Muted life for fear of a terrifying death—all death is terrifying—is well documented. The defeatism of which we speak courses through all art and science, determining subject matter. All intellectual pursuits thus far, in East and West alike, have been largely stopgap measures, so much fiddling while Rome burns, that is, while people line up one after another to die. Adhering to a defeatist position, practitioners of every discipline, whether focused on figuring out life or on amusing or intriguing those who have life, stop before they ever reach the point of becoming radical, so convinced are they that we are destined to die. The defeatists are everywhere. Within the life sciences, they try to cure the human body or figure it out such as they find it to be, never attempting to reconfigure it altogether, never thinking to reorder the body radically so that it might elude mortality. Because most life scientists have, along with everyone else, dismissed out of hand any thought of a possible fundamental reordering of the body, they are at a loss as to how to judge the import of human cloning, for example, a method through which the body could conceivably be reconfigured for the better.

Researchers work together but do not pitch in to attack problems as fervently as they would if they felt their lives depended on it. The species deserves some credit for having sought to maintain a historical continuity, but too often one finds, as a result of haphazard or negligible follow-up, odd breaks in this supposed continuity; all too frequently, research initiatives are abandoned once their initial supporters have disappeared. Coordinating research projects from diverse fields requires knowing where to place the emphasis, and hardly anyone knows how to do this in our time. Even on those rare occasions when the emphasis has been rightly placed, that emphasis has not been sufficiently emphatic. Insensitive to its own immediate needs, to the nature of itself as the central problem, our species—mostly represented by those who speak the loudest or the longest—is so unboundedly proud of having built the cart that it permanently, in an ongoing fit of mad harnessing, features it before the horse. The horse: the animate. The cart: culture, be it modern or postmodern.

That human life is expendable as a matter of course, that we are mortal, that life comes thus blighted as a matter of fact, as a matter of hideously brutal fact, is antithetical to any ethics putting the highest value of all on the preserving of life. An ethics that fails to take a stand against what counters it must be seen to have been subverted by it. It is illogical (and arguably unethical) for an ethical system that values life not to see mortality as fundamentally unethical. In thus arguing it would seem that you wish to make a mockery of our ethics, a critic might reply. There is death and then there is death. That life must not be extinguished, yes, that is our teaching. But when it comes to mortality itself, to try to uphold that standard would be equivalent to trying to stop a flood with a finger in the dam. No, no, one must give up on that score. And so, most ethical codes simply put to one side the issue of mortality and proceed to go on, we put it to you, quite unrealistically from there, starting off on the thither side of the crucial fact, and so, going along always to one side of the facts as they stand.

An ethics that permits no category of event, not even mortality, to be set apart for special treatment, and that considers there to be nothing more unethical than that we are required to be mortal shall be called a *crisis ethics*. Three decades ago, by wedding the word *reversible* with the term *destiny*, a supposedly set-in-stone sequence of events, we announced a war on mortality. Reversible destiny was our first step into a crisis ethics. What if it turned out that to be mortal was not an essential condition of our species? To repeat in a slightly different way what people are so unused to hearing: What if it turned out that members of our species were not forever slated to be mortal? Another way to read reversible destiny—a less radical way, but for some people, we are given to understand, a perhaps less terrifying and therefore more inviting way—is as an open challenge to our species to reinvent itself and to desist from foreclosing on any possibility, even those our contemporaries judge to be impossible.

If you want to do the impossible, should you be desirous of

tilting at windmills, why not build to your own specifications the windmills at which you wish to tilt? In the spirit of always taking things further, a spirit characteristic of those desiring to do the impossible, why not indeed build the whole of the world in which those windmills tilt? And furthermore still, why not build windmills that tilt back toward you knowingly and informatively? That is to say, first off, that we have seen our contemporaries looking at the two of us as if we were Don Quixotes. And indeed we tip our hats to a comparable indomitableness, even as we rush to contrast our impossibilities with his. For our part, we never approach anything impossible unless the setup is right. A right setup frames actions; within a right setup actions become more readily analyzable, repeatable, and able to be followed up on. We ask only that enormous sums of money be spent on constructing the world as a tactically posed surrounding for the benefit of the body. A procedural constructing of the world will constitute a way for our species to take evolution into its own hands. In some sense, any of the coordinating skills our species has been able to count as its own would have, prior to their having been acquired, been thought to be impossible.

A ruling concern is that nothing conceivably belonging in the picture (to be painted of the world) be left out of it. If bound to err one is, then choose always, when judging what merits inclusion, to err in the direction of being overly inclusive. When organisms-persons are the subject of study, that they subsist within architectural environments ought not to be ignored; specific features of environments, along with interactions they invite, belong in the picture. This emphasis on an all-inclusiveness, an inclination to attend to everything, naturally leads to more specificity, a searching out of exact placements of, and uses for, the elements and features of architectural environments.

Consider this: *An organism-person allied with, in close corre-*

spondence with, surroundings that guide skillful coordination of bodily actions ought to be able to escape so-called human destiny, the as-if-ordained downhill course of things. Not only will houses and towns that architecturally guide and sustain an organism-person help her to compose, execute, and coordinate actions more skillfully than was ever before thought to be possible, they will also automatically enlist her in a thoroughgoing architectural questioning of the purpose of the species. An architecturally guided and sustained organism-person should then be able to reverse that destiny known to have been the lot of billions of other members of her species; when it becomes possible for an organism-person simply to go on indefinitely, a reversible destiny shall have been achieved.

If you say no, or yes, to this automatically, who are you, then, and where does it get you?

Architecture is the greatest tool available to our species, both for figuring itself out and for constructing itself differently. For the crisis ethicist, the judge and the jury, the witnesses and their testimonies, the everything, is this body that each of us, in living, has in evidence. And the body, a complex organism that is always in the process of reading surroundings, needs to be defined together with that within which it moves; peering at it from the other way around, the surroundings need to be defined together with bodies moving within them.

To repeat: have the architectural surroundings themselves, by virtue of how they are formed, pose questions directly to the body. The unit for consideration, that which is to be measured and assessed, should be the body taken together with its surroundings. How to put all that one is as a body to best use becomes the chief ethical concern. Lives should be lived as case studies, and surely not isolated ones. No one should consider herself a finished product or a non-puzzle; everyone should live as a self-marmot (self-guinea pig). Self-marmots will act as coordinators that keep discoveries from all fields of research actively in the arena. A self-marmot's urge to assemble knowledge, to effect a living synthesis, will be sparked by a recognition of the state of emergency in which she is doomed to live. Research should no longer be done off to one side, in a school, a library, a laboratory. Where one lives needs to become a laboratory for researching, for mapping directly, the living body itself, oneself as world-forming inhabitant.

What then is preventing us from inventing ourselves further? The answer comes quickly: the species has not yet learned how to have its members pull together to work communally at the same time they continue to form themselves as separate individuals. The species is in need of a common purpose, fueled by a sharp sense of a shared plight, and a concerted communal effort to address this purpose. And this is so, despite the fact that every individual has been formed communally, and that therefore all actions have communal echoes and repercussions (this is easily proven). For members of our species to arrive at having a great many more than the paltry sum of possibilities that is usually their due, there needs to be a communal devising, selecting, and combining of techniques that will strengthen organisms-persons and help them to regenerate themselves; results need to be pooled and compared.

To be insisted on: sentience assembles its swerving suite of cognizing stances depending on how the body disports itself—the whole of this text will prove this statement. Therefore, architecture ought to be designed for actions it invites. Theoretical constructs as to the nature of person can be assessed in a thoroughgoing manner through—and, in the end, only through—architectural construction.

Economic priority should be given to the resolving of existential puzzles: What is this species in the first place? What lives and what dies? It is admittedly costly for our species to ask questions of itself through architecture, particularly if one determines it to be necessary to devote an entire room to the posing of a single question, or, for that matter, if it should turn out that two rooms are needed for that purpose, or even if the testing of a single hypothesis might necessitate that an entire house (or a city) be constructed. But if this is how and from where the answers can come at last, why worry over the expense?

Architectural Body

1
Organism That Persons

Born into a new territory, and that territory is myself as organism. There is no place to go but here. Each organism that persons finds the new territory that is itself, and, having found it, adjusts it. This is so only if systematically organized events, fields in which relations among events have some degree of order, can count as territories. An organism-person-environment has given birth to an organism-person-environment.

The organism we are speaking of persons the world; other types of organisms dog, giraffe, or cockroach the world. While members of lower species routinely produce behavior that is true to type, the organism that persons, not always able to summon up all it must to produce a person, has a higher probability of failure. Various instances of an organism's having behaved as a person, many in succession, sum up as a person. It may seem that an organism has a person with which it is associated, but rather than actually having a person, an organism has a long-term association only with behaving as a person. Who has been accepted as a person by other persons is really nothing more than the set of ways an organism that persons behaves.

The momentum an organism is able to gain on being a person, or rather, on behaving as one—that set of conditions, born of actions taken, that makes person-formation possible— depends directly on how it positions its body. Surroundings invite, provoke, and entice persons to perform actions, and the enacting motions of these actions not only serve up alternate vantage points but also inevitably shift sense organs about. The shifting about of the sense organs naturally affects how a person fields her surroundings and has much to do with what of the surroundings ends up standing for or approximating *the surroundings.*

This that is I—an organism behaving as a person—ascribes. I do so ascribe. Organisms deploy; (organisms behaving as) persons ascribe. Not enough information on what obtains between organism and person has been collected, and the ebb and flow of each entity of this dynamic two-in-one duo remains uncharted. Any term that purports to reveal the dynamics of person formation but which fails to suggest the body's intricate relation to the environment muddies the view. Terms such as *ego, consciousness,* and *psyche,* losing the body as they do, lack those air passages through which the body draws in atmospheric wherewithal.

Close observations have yet to be made of the effect of type of habitation on persons. Those who would minutely observe the effect of habitation on human beings must begin to discern how and why surroundings give or withhold from organisms of the type that can person the means to behave as persons. Even as the concept of person can stay put (everyone knows what a person is), it needs to be greatly dilated (particularly within a book entitled *Architectural Body*). We have adopted the admittedly clumsy term "organism that persons" because it portrays persons as being intermittent and transitory outcomes of coordinated forming rather than honest-to-goodness entities; now that we have launched the term, we use the following less cumbersome terms synonymously with it: body, body-proper, human being, organism, organism-person, person. When studying what goes on between the body-proper and its surroundings, it will be necessary to consider the extent to which persons are behavioral subsets of the organisms from which they emanate and out of which they compose themselves as agents of action. The organism that persons is the first step on the path to the architectural body.

Or neonates come equipped with set-to-go architectural bodies that their first movements activate and help shape—each newborn organism-person-environment an Atlas shouldering the world in its entirety. The toddler, taking its first steps as an organism that persons, drags its whole world along as pull-toy (architectural body).

Although finding where organism leaves off and person begins would seem an impossible task, keeping the question starkly unresolved will most likely provide the best view of what is in play. With less glossing and less generalizing going on, there are increases in both overall tentativeness of the situation and in a free-ranging on-the-spot observing that leads to direct mapping. Good scout that a human being is, ever bent on making do, on glossing interrupted melodies into tunes, she takes scattered moments of an organism's (herself) behaving as a person and smooths them into a whole, herself. D. W. Winnicott's principle of "good enough" holds not only for mothers (according to Winnicott, any mother who is genuinely able to be there for her baby is a "good enough" mother) but also for persons (as we see it, any organism that genuinely exhibits person behavior is a "good enough" person).

An integrally intelligent whole, always capable of bringing conscious reflection into the mix, the organism-person feels and thinks its (way through an) environment. Upon its being granted that each person acts within her environment as a thinking body—nerve tissue can be found throughout the body, the neuromuscular system can coordinate itself to act thoughtfully, and each organ acts "knowledgeably" within its own domain—architecture then looms large as a great aid to critical thinking. Architecture's task is to mete out the world in such a way that it might be reflected on body-wide. And what does thinking—global, body-wide thinking—need? Thinking surely needs perseverance in the matter at hand, the continual pursuing of that which perplexes, a coming at it and to it from all sides. And when it comes to a thinking that takes place in the round, to reflecting or musing *environmentally*, that would seem to require having something there to be returned to and entered at least twice, a stream (a host of streams) into which, as it flows fixedly as itself, one can set foot more than once. Heraclitus points out the impossibility of this. He correctly maintains that nothing stays in place as place but flux. No two moments have identical streams in which to rest a weary foot and wiggle one's toes. For that matter, no two moments offer up an identical foot for insertion into a cooling stream. Even so, for the figuring out of this or that conundrum, thinking does require there to be a fastening onto an area of consideration and a holding steady, a relative staying in place—and this is what we introduce the architectural body into the world to achieve.

A taking shape of surrounds and bodies and organisms and persons occurs intermixedly. Logic would want to get in there with a knife and cut them apart. Although we are utterly dependent on the force of logic prior to constructing the surrounds that will test our hypotheses, we will say no to logic and resist making incisions and separating the probably inseparable. All the linking and enclosing, an it (think of this as an autopoietic system if you like) that starts as enclosed and then goes about enclosing itself—all of that needs to be picked up as an organism-like whole, kicking and screaming, alive with process, emphatically, and urgently rushed into a supporting context of embedded procedures.

2
Landing Sites

Were nothing being apportioned out, no world could form. What is being apportioned out, no one is able to say. That which is being apportioned out is in the process of landing. To be apportioned out involves being cognizant of sites. To be cognizant of a site amounts to having greeted it in some manner or to having in some way landed on it. There is that which gets apportioned out as the world. There is an apportioning out that can register and an apportioning out that happens more indeterminately. A systematic approximating of how things are apportioned out should be possible.

The body is sited. As that which initiates pointing, selecting, electing, determining, and considering, it may be said to originate (read *co-originate*) all sites. Organism-person-environment consists of sites and would-be sites. An organism-person, a sited body, lives as one site that is composed of many sites. One can, for example, consider one's arms and legs to be part of a single site (the body) or elect them to be two sites (an upper-appendages realm and a lower-appendages one) or four (two upper and two lower appendages) or twenty-four or more sites (two arms having a total of ten fingers, and two legs with ten toes in all).

∞

"If persons are sited, why do philosophers inquiring into what constitutes a person, or, for that matter, into the nature of mind, rarely, if ever, factor this in?"

"Philosophers considering persons as sites would be obliged

to develop a person architectonics. They would, I am afraid, have to turn themselves into architects of sorts."

"First off, might not the world exist so that everyone may turn into an architect? Contemporary philosophers who insist on remaining within the narrow confines of their discipline risk not being able to frame questions as broadly as necessary and thus jeopardize the logical basis of their inquiry. Does anyone really believe that a person could ever be figured out as such in the abstract?"

Designating the "coming alive" for sentience—as sentience?!—of anything whatsoever, including even the most fleeting sensations, a landing site is but a neutral marker, a simple taking note of, nothing more. When how the world is apportioned out is translated into landing sites, all stays the same, touched but untouched. A person parses the world at any given instant into particular distributions of landing sites, or better, an organism-person-environment can be parsed into these distributions; it is of great use, we hope to demonstrate, to think of the world as reduced to these distributions, these parsings, these arrays, and nothing more. This way what goes on as the world, the world taken all together, all inhabitants included, can be kept track of and looked into with a minimal amount of speculation as to what's in play. If we don't know what is being distributed, let us simply stay with the fact that distributions of some order are underway. We may not yet know how we are connected to the world, but we do know that we are. Let us be precise or suitably imprecise about what we do know so far.

Adopting as a theoretical posit the concept of a landing site, we seek to make and keep explicit an otherwise hidden-in-plain-sight constant of awareness: all things and events have specific positionings. Intent on tracking a person's apportioning out of thinking-feeling to form a world that she then interacts with, and wondering whether it is at all valid to think of a "depositing" of sited awareness everywhere around one, we establish a schematic domain of *landing sites.*

A multiple, complex siting process or procedure would seem to be in effect as organism-person-environment; or posing it more neutrally, the world one finds in place lends itself to being mapped by means of a multiple, complex siting process or procedure. Human action depends on an attributing of sites and takes place in large part through sequences of sitings. In determining her surroundings, a person proceeds by registering a "this here" and a "that there" and a "more of this here" and a "more of that there." In fielding her surroundings, she makes use of cues from the environment to assign volume and a host of particulars to world and to body, complying with what comes her way as best she can. Her fielding of her surroundings never ceases, continuing even in sleep. Whatever comes up in the course of this fielding should be considered a landing site.

We start off by thinking of world-construction as involving three different ways to land as a site. Every landing-site configuration—that is, every instance of the world—involves all three ways of landing as a site. A *perceptual landing site* lands narrowly as an immediate and direct response to a probable existent, a bit of reporting on what presents itself. An *imaging landing site* lands widely and in an un-pinpointing way, dancing attendance on the perceptual landing site, responding indirectly and diffusely to whatever the latter leaves unprocessed. Apeing a perceptual landing site's direct response to a probable existent, it keeps faith with and firms up a reporting impetus underway. Usually this mimicking landing site, a gloss instrumental in its coming to seem that nothing has escaped attention, simply goes about indirectly coming up with more of the same, making it appear that direct responding to probable existents covers a wider area and has a longer-lasting effect than it actually does. But an imaging landing site can also, absent perceptual landing sites, when a sensory modality has closed down, suggest itself to be a direct response that initiates a report, thus turning itself for all intents and purposes into a perceptual landing site (witness the Karl Dahlke report a few pages further along). Imaging landing sites can also, in response to an indeterminate probable existent, simply come forward as a portion of sited awareness that remains diffuse, thus presenting areas of world without mimicking anything at all; to demonstrate this look off into thin air. A *dimensionalizing landing site* lands simultaneously narrowly and tightly and widely and diffusely, combining the qualities of a perceptual landing site with those of an imaging one, coupling and coordinating direct responses with indirect ones, the formed with the formless. Attaching a grappling hook of a perceptual landing site to a vaguely sketched-in rope of an imaging landing site, a dimensionalizing landing site, in landing, hooks onto the environment to gain traction on it. With the hook-and-rope ensemble flung out and an availing surface caught hold of, there comes to be an as-if-tugging-back-to-the-body that conveys a sense of (kinesthetic) depth.

Defining features (perceptual landing sites), plus all the imaging that bounces off that which surrounds a person (imaging landing sites), plus guesses and judgments as to how elements of the surroundings are positioned (dimensionalizing landing sites) fabricate a world or suffice to map one. Landing sites dissolve into each other, or abut, or overlap, or nest within one another.

Every square foot or every square nanometer of organism-person-environment occasions a landing site. Surroundings are for a person what comes of her ubiquitous siting; that is to say, they exist as a result of her having dispersed landing sites ubiquitously within a circumscribed area, leaving no square nanometer uncovered. Fielding the surroundings, distributing sentience in specific ways to do this, one lets loose ubiquitous sitings or landing-site configurations which permeate and supplant one another in rapid succession. Every surroundings elicits from those within it a characteristic series of ubiquitous sitings or landing-site configurations.

Landing sites abound within landing sites. Anything perceived can count as both a landing site in and of itself and as part of a larger landing site. The corner of a desk can be taken as a full-fledged landing site, even while subsisting as part of the landing site holding and portraying the desk as a whole. The taking of a particular expanse or event to be a landing site happens in a flash; over in a flash; these events that are decision-like but far from being decisions yield to whatever can come next. A bit of substance, a segment of atmosphere, an audible anything, a whiff of something, whatever someone notices can be declared either a whole landing site or part of one, or both of these at once. Through landing-site configurations, organism-person-environment takes hold and holds forth.

Accepting that the world can be sorted out, at each instant, into only a limited number of landing sites that can readily be kept track of and maneuvering with this information without trying to overreach it amounts to taking a neutral stance. A landing-site configuration can, then, be thought of as a heuristic device with which to leaf through the universe, never mind that it is unpaginated. This heuristic device, a set of apportionings-out capable of reading what else has been and is being apportioned out, leafs through the universe to determine its arrangement and its contingencies. Leafing through a universe turns it into the world.

Perceptual Landing Sites

Theoretically, what counts as the world might be divided into an infinite number of specific locatings or focal areas of awareness, but various studies have shown that, at any given moment, the world consists, for a person, of only a limited number of activated regions or focal hubs of activity.* The continual, albeit episodic, designating of this or that as here or there is not routinely included in this small limit-group of focal notings, but inasmuch as we have in this the originator, or more accurately co-originator, of all regions and hubs, it—this that apportions out—merits inclusion as a member. In any event, one finds a constant selecting of discrete groups of designated areas, with yet other groups in the offing. All points or areas of focus, that is, all designated areas of specified activity, count as perceptual landing sites (visual, aural, tactile, olfactory, proprioceptive, kinesthetic, somaesthetic [pain]).

Perceptual landing sites occur always in sets—a flock of birds flying in formation. With every move she makes, a person disperses her perceptual landing sites differently. Resting within or overlapping one another, they are hard to pin down as to size. Should, however, there be a fairly continual distinguishing of a focal area of activity, a definite size might provisionally be accorded a member of the set. Upon this happening, there would surface the illusion that one had met with that rare, nonexistent bird: the lone perceptual landing site.

Perceptual landing sites pop up on demand, converging upon whatever is around to be landed on. All singled-out elements of surrounding surfaces: perceptual landing sites. Even a mere intimation of a singling-out equals having been landed

*George A. Miller, "The Magical Number Seven, Plus or Minus Two: Some Limits on Our Capacity for Processing Information," *Psychological Review* 63 (1956): 81–97; Zenon W. Pylyshyn, "Visual Indexes, Preconceptual Objects, Situated Vision," *Cognition* 80 (June 2001): 127–58.

on and sited. Repeated singlings-out bring the world into existence in all its features. I assign a perceptual landing site to this. Or does it take shape by means of many sites of this type? A shape may be formed first as one perceptual landing site and then considered to be defined by ten, after which it might be judged to have been defined by one hundred or any number of such sites, landing sites that are "direct hits." Because sites abound within sites, and because any X that is not a site is a would-be one, the assigning of perceptual landing sites can only be carried out hazily and tentatively. That it is not possible to determine the number of perceptual landing sites involved in something's coming to be perceived may be viewed as a drawback to the system we propose, yet it need not be a matter of great concern. Regardless of the softness of numbers assigned, despite the inevitable imprecision, perceptual landing sites, whatever their number, always, by definition, register accurately enough features and elements of the circumstances they have been dispersed to record.

Were there no perceptual landing sites, there could be no organism-person that is a body. Perceptual landing sites serve up the initiating site of all sites, the basically fixed but constantly changing kinesthetic-proprioceptive schema of body that keeps a person always kinesthetically grounded and figured and configured. Nothing happens without kinesthetic instigation, corporeal proddings. All events have palpably active starts, stops, and turnabouts and kinesthetic repercussions. A mobile and sculpted medium of locatings or of events composed of kinesthetic- and proprioceptive-perceptual landing sites animates the show from within and in great measure runs it.

Imaging Landing Sites

To honor and mark that it is unquestionably the case that landing-site dispersal occurs within the context of an imaging capability, as well as to account for this capability within the information management system that landing-site theory, still in its infancy, apparently engenders, we have taken to referring to ubiquitous emissaries of this capability as imaging landing sites. An area not captured by perceptual landing sites, accorded no points of focus or touchdown points of awareness, does not simply go blank or vanish; instead, it—a looming non-focused-upon area—far from bowing out of the picture or leaving great gaps in it, gets continually supplied, or roughed in, or approximated, by imaging landing sites.

Imaging, integral to a person's forming of the world, gets staked out and maintained by landing sites that fill in gaps in the world or "generalize" it. Imaging landing sites hover around, pick up on, and emulate qualities or features that perceptual landing sites highlight. Taking off from perceptual landing sites (actual points of focus), imaging landing sites (generalizing factors) extend and diffuse surfaces and volumes. Imaging landing sites enlarge the areas over which qualities hold sway. In the course of producing what they produce, they bruit this about: "Have there be more of this here and around here." The picture that emerges is a far cry from the mosaic of empiricists, with its standard same-sized tiles of sensation. Instead of a mosaic of registerings, we have a shifting-about patchwork quilt of registerings and quasi-registerings. We have a patchwork quilt that never stays the same. Palimpsests of quilts of patchworked registerings and quasi-registerings on the move; registerings and quasi-registerings slipping under and over one another, replacing one another. Imaging landing sites: quasi-registerings.

Amorphous accordings of more information than is directly supplied, imaging landing sites exist as even less discrete patches of world than perceptual landing sites. Blending the surroundings and blending into the surroundings, they have hardly any shape at all and perhaps had best be spoken of as shapeless; even so, they help define the shapes of the objects of the world. Imaging landing sites are not even of an indeterminate size; they are, instead, possibly without scale. This does not mean that they have no part in recording scale. They fall in line with whatever perceptual landing sites (and dimensionalizing landing sites) determine the measure of things to be. What they mete out in this regard gets abundantly meted out in the spirit of a grand, continual, cooperative gesture toward getting a world to form (out of the universe).

And where might imaging landing sites lie? Where do any landing sites lie? Might not all landing sites lie within (or throughout) an imaging domain of sorts? If so, how what transpires originates in imaging has yet to be determined. Surely imaging capability derives from a mobile and sculpted medium of locatings composed, for a start, of kinesthetic and tactile landing sites, the human body. In any event, a part of the whole exists as imaging. Imaging landing sites eventuate not only in patches that fill in and finish the world but also in all manner of figural event. We believe that the resolving of these matters requires the construction of complex measuring and tracking devices, constructions by which to gain perspective on human functioning and separate out its component factors.

Persons, then, field their surroundings kinesthetically, tactilely, visually, aurally, olfactorily, and gustatorily all at once, with each modality having a direct or perceptual component and an indirect or imaging one. For example, within the perceptual array, objects that are not touched have no immediate tactile component; these might be said to have, instead, a mediate one, a tactile-*imaging* component that portrays how objects are *likely to feel* to the touch. Tactile-imaging landing sites confer on the world a sense of texture or of nascent texture. All perceptual landing sites have corresponding imaging landing sites; visual landing sites have corresponding sets of visual-*imaging* landing sites, aural landing sites have corresponding sets of aural-*imaging* landing sites, and so on. We have taken to referring to kinesthetic-*imaging* landing sites as ambient-kinesthetic landing sites or as ambient kinesthesia. We plan to study in a later work the extent to which sited awareness is imbued with an ambient kinesthesia.

Not only do imaging landing sites extend perceptual landing sites, continually providing "more of the same" as they hover about them and emulate qualities and features they incarnate as or capture, they can unprompted imitate these direct responses to probable existents well enough to act as stand-ins for them. Although much about the following account remains unresolved, it being after all an isolated case, anecdotal and un-followed-up-on, we present it here for three reasons: it demonstrates well the stand-in capacity of an imaging landing site; it has something to contribute to our difficult-to-put-together concept of a dimensionalizing landing site; and it gives an undistorted view of imaging capacity, leaving it untouched, an open question, even as it shows how in some way all depends on it.

Recounting how he was able to perform the amazing feat of solving the polyomino puzzle, a mapping puzzle about bordering territories that had gone unsolved for several decades, Karl Dahlke, the blind mathematician, reviewed the steps he had taken. He remembers having cut a piece of cardboard into twenty identical pieces, polyominos, and then having spent time positioning them in relation to one another. Next, he left off working with the physical pieces and began instead to

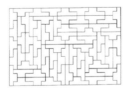

POLYOMINO PUZZLE

visualize a large, brown board that stood right in front of him ready to have shiny, white polyominos placed upon it. Choosing a corner from which to begin, he affixed piece after piece to the board, finding how best to position each one so as to come up with a solution; he continued doing this until the number of pieces affixed to the board exceeded his capacity to remember—that is, until he began, as he put it, "to run out of memory"—at which point, using Lego blocks, he constructed a model of what he had visualized. When questioned about the elements of his visualization, he replied as follows:

> Come to think of it, the puzzle pieces were three-dimensional or had some three-dimensionality to them . . . and this was so despite the fact that I was seeking to solve a puzzle of two-dimensional space. This is a false artifact, I guess, having to do with the way my touch can be of use in positioning pieces. Memory also plays a part in it. My early memories of three-dimensionality during the years when I still had sight. . . . And you ask about the density of the visualized pieces? I would say they have the same density in the visualization as I feel them to have when I touch them—now that of the cardboard pieces and now that of the Lego blocks, at times turning out to be a mixture of the two. And how thick is the board to which I affix the puzzle pieces? It needs to be as thin as possible, for it is there only as a . . . what shall I say, I put it to use only as a memory expander. But I cannot repeat often enough: Choosing carefully the corner from which to begin is critically important.*

Dahlke recalls having spent hour upon hour placing shiny, white polyominos into position upon a thin, brown board. Working in this way, he could try polyominos out in various

*Karl Dahlke, interview, April 21, 1989.

positions within the group he had assembled, even while he was strolling across campus, soaking in a tub, or resting in bed. He would go on deliberating and, in his words, "seeing-touching along," until he grew tired, at which point he would promptly shut off the lights as it were and go to sleep. Remarkably, when he awoke, the puzzle pieces were exactly as he had left them. The puzzle was always there as he had thus far worked it out.

There can be no doubt that Dahlke's picturing of the polyomino puzzle involves no visual perceptual landing sites. He is certainly not issuing direct responses to probable existents. Even so, puzzle pieces need to be given definite shapes and precisely positioned, and both these tasks are, by definition, specific to perceptual landing sites. This leads us to conclude that imaging landing sites act, for Dahlke, as stand-ins for visual perceptual ones. We find these mimics keying polyominos or salient features of polyominos into position in ways more in keeping with events and actions of a seen world than an imaged one. How do Dahlke's imaging landing sites succeed in plausibly presenting themselves as direct responses to puzzle pieces?

It is only in special circumstances that an imaging landing site can take on all of, or nearly all of, the characteristics of a perceptual landing site, and Dahlke would seem to have instinctively arrived at having fashioned such circumstances for himself. One thing we can be certain of is that Dahlke's imaging landing sites that parade as perceptual landing sites could never field the external world as the latter do. Nonetheless, he is able to sharpen their focus and get them to deliver up to him results most people can only get from perceptual landing sites. He does this, we believe, by being willing to reduce the whole of his surroundings down to a thin, brown board—a focused-in world to which to attend. He reduces ambient light and air and the whole field of probable existents to but a single object with minimal breadth and expanse that has been, it appears, apportioned out to hold precisely twenty polyominos of a particular yet hard-to-specify size. Dahlke puts this object, which we would be tempted to call a critical holder (see chapter 8), in place as a memory expander. Is it only in a context as limited as this, one as pointedly reined in as this, that imaging landing sites can perfectly mimic perceptual ones?

When Dahlke reduces his surroundings, at least as far as visual perception is concerned, to a thin, brown board, what makes his imaging landing sites able to come alive as perceptual ones? An imager of a puzzle or of, for that matter, anything at all usually has a wide-open choice as to where within sited awareness to place what is imaged. Imaging thus comes with a whole host of would-be sites to be imaged. The more ambiguous the surroundings, the greater the number of imaging landing sites that will be needed for making determinations and giving things shape. Ambiguous surroundings tap an imager's resources or energy supply on two counts: first, because a large number of imaging landing sites will need to be churned out, and second, because a great deal of short-term memory will have to be used to keep track of what these landing sites have surfaced as.

While for computers—and Dahlke's term, "memory expander," does seem to have originated in computer lingo— memory expansion can be effected through the deletion of data, the insertion of additional hardware for increased storage capacity and more processing power, or the swapping out of different storage or processing areas; in human beings, memory (short-term) expansion can be effected only through a provisional striking out of data that translates into a freeing up of memory space, that is through reducing memory requirements for one task so that the requirements of another task can be met. A certain over-allness, what might otherwise be seen to take up most of short-term memory, and which even in ordinary circumstances must be seen to put an enormous strain on imaging or generalizing power, has been cut short, reduced back to a thin, brown board—a board that conveniently stays parallel to the imager's forehead no matter which way he moves. Now Dahlke can concentrate on imaging-remembering what polyominos he put where. A great reduction in one area has made it possible for there to be a great expansion (of imaging power) in another.*

When queried further, Dahlke does admit there to be a bit of ambient distance between the part of himself that initiates the thing-like events he uses as puzzle pieces, his landing sites, and the board upon which he will, by means of imaging landing sites, place polyominos and to which he will find himself, again by means of imaging landing sites, frequently returning. He also remembers there to have been now and then a vague hand-like event affixing the pieces to the board.

The external world, which is always there to supply what one might otherwise feel obliged to remember, and thus frees memory for matters other than keeping track of the immediate surroundings, might qualify as a memory expander for the sighted. Memory is freed up when one no longer needs to remember what is perceived because one is simply able to revisit it, and this, by most accounts, is what the external world has to offer. Upon entering a room, a person begins dispersing perceptual landing sites to record its features. One may not know what one first noticed, where one's reading of one's surroundings began, but one of course must and does begin somewhere. It is, in any event, in the nature of actions within surroundings to have beginning, middle, and end points and

*For more on how reduction leads to expansion, see Arakawa and Madeline Gins, "Expansion and Reduction—Meaning of Scale," subdivision no. 6 of *The Mechanism of Meaning* (New York: Abbeville Press, 1988).

for chosen beginning, middle, and end points to be places that are stable enough to invite return visits. That it is able to be returned to makes something's existence more probable. Hence, Dahlke speaks of how critically important choosing where to begin is. His careful constructing of a starting point would seem to be a way for him to transform his drastically reduced surroundings into an as-if external world. We think this would remain true even if upon further questioning Dahlke were to reveal that it was not the whole setup for the polyomino puzzle but the puzzle itself that required a focused beginning. We can unhesitatingly assert this because we have come to see that to carry imitating of a perceptual landing site to exquisite lengths, that which disperses mimicking sites needs first of all to mimic a probable existent on which to land; if he is to make his world be as-if external, endowing it with probable existence, Dahlke must boldly mark a beginning place that can be revisited.

It is fair to say that Dahlke has never seen a polyomino. It should probably be assumed that for the solving of this puzzle he "sees" the polyomino in whatever form it is most convenient for him to have it. It is a compromise solution whose startling accuracy is sufficient to allow the puzzle to be solved. He manufactures polyominos out of the whole cloth of his sited awareness; we will bring up more of what goes into their manufacture when, in the next section, we discuss dimensionalizing landing sites; neither we nor anyone else is prepared at this time in history to go into the whole of this whole cloth. But what are these polyominos? What is a polyomino of Dahlke's manufacture made of? An imaging landing site that suddenly has a sharp face, a face suddenly in focus, all of a sudden a new facet? Or is this polyomino that he can affix to the board a sculpted flake of the crust of some cloud that has grown to be bread-like? Whatever else this is, it is a class of long-lasting imaging landing site able to remain in place long enough for other imaging landing sites to visit it. When Dahlke thinks he has solved a section of the puzzle, say, one-fourth of it, that group of polyominos, those several imaging landing sites parading as perceptual ones, coalesce into a single larger imaging landing site that can, in its guise of probable existent, be revisited. We leave it to the reader to imagine the sound with which imaging landing sites assume their positions upon the thinnest of thin boards to which they flock even as their source models perceptual landing sites.

The most highly probable existent or landing site in all that Dahlke recounts would have to be Dahlke himself. In any event, although Dahlke's marvelously intensified or souped-up image, his precise picturing of the polyomino puzzle, a special order of precision-held image that marvelously permits shiftings-about and change, takes place through imaging, and can therefore be said to exist in the realm of imaging, it certainly cannot be said to be completely without perceptual landing sites. In addition to having locatings and notings throughout his body (kinesthetic perceptual landing sites) and sounds and odors coming at him from every direction (aural and olfactory perceptual landing sites), Dahlke feels feet in shoes and shoes on terrain, clothing wherever it touches his skin; sitting upon a chair, he feels it along his back and arms and across his bottom, or lying upon a bed, his head upon a plumped pillow, he feels the cushioning surface along his back, neck, and head, or along the front of his body, or along one side of his body (tactile perceptual landing sites all). Any tactile landing site stirs up around itself kinesthetic flickerings, nudgings, and push-pull-cracklings. Dahlke's precisely positioned puzzle that would seem to be all made of imaging landing sites has, then, a firm basis in perceptual landing sites as well. Never to be overlooked: there is a great deal more to imaging than imaging alone.

Dimensionalizing Landing Sites

Acknowledging that a person experiences not only sites but also depths, we posit a composite landing site (a landing-site "molecule" formed of the two landing-site "atoms" we have named perceptual and imaging). A dimensionalizing landing site registers location and position relative to the body. Building, assessing, and reading volume and dimension, dimensionalizing landing sites "engineer" depth and effect the siting of sites. These sites register and determine the bounds and shapes of the environment.

A chair as pictured or held in place by perceptual landing sites (direct perception) with the assistance of imaging landing sites (indirect or imitative perception) has for its perceiver a distinct position in relation to everything else in the room—the work of dimensionalizing landing sites (part direct, part indirect perception).

Think of the part that judgments of dimension play in Dahlke's surprisingly precise picturing of the polyomino puzzle. He uses tactile and kinesthetic perceptual landing sites to add depth to a visualized image. Transposing how, in sum, the puzzle pieces felt to his touch as he held them at various angles and moved his fingers over them, he endows the imaged pieces with some solidity, a burgeoning hint of three-dimensionality. Dimensionalizing is conducted cross-modally, as are all the actions of a person. It has been shown that the illusion generated by the Ames room—giant boy, tiny adult—vanishes when the viewer, armed with a stick so as to probe the room's interior, learns tactilely and kinesthetically that the floor slopes, and gathers that what she has imaged to be an ordinary room is anything but ordinary.

The best way to get a sense of how dimensionalizing landing sites function is to think of what happens when they are missing or insufficiently arrayed. Everyone has had the experience of feeling like an idiot when stubbing her toe. The necessary dimensionalizing landing sites were not in place, depth was not inserted where it needed to be.

A Neutral Zone of Emphasis

Think of a nod of recognition to position and substance, a nod that recognizes where and what and nothing more. A dispersion of landing sites: a scattering of nods that everywhere notes positionings. A landing-site configuration forms, as a heuristic device, when the continual symbolizing of a symbolizing creature—when that which can, in effect, make a metaphor or symbol of anything—becomes slightly muted or is put on hold for a bit; the symbolizing creature becomes a landing-site coordinating creature. The tense of landing sites holds as that split second of muting whose instantaneous time span lasts only long enough for basic positionings to be registered. Providing a neutral zone of emphasis, landing sites simply bypass subject-object distinctions. Landing site: a muted symbol, or one—but inseparable from all others—event-marker in and of the event-fabric that is organism-person-environment.

A neutral stance asks that nonresolvable issues be kept on hold—fluidly and flexibly on hold—right out there in the world where they occur; it asks as well that they be held open and be made to open still further to yield additional information about what is at issue. Landing sites deliver an on-the-spot data management system. Information management—that is what landing sites are set up to do. On-the-spot data managing is now within everyone's reach.

3
Architecture as Hypothesis

Here is what architecture means to us: *a tentative constructing toward a holding in place.* Walk into this building and you walk into a purposeful guess. The built world floats a hypothesis or two as to how and by what the apportioned out comes to be everywhere, the everywhere.

ARAKAWA: Here is the house we were telling you about.

ANGELA: I don't see any house here.

GINS: Granted this is not what in our time most people dream of coming home to.

ROBERT: This heap?

GINS: Yes, a low pile of material that covers a fairly vast area.

ANGELA: Are we at a dump? This low pile covering a vast area.

GINS: What you take to be a pile of junk ranges in height from three to eleven inches. It measures close to 2,400 square feet—or 2,900 square feet if you include the courtyard.

ROBERT: Courtyard?

GINS: The shining part in the middle that has a lot of green around it.

ANGELA: That's hilarious. Your house is shorter than its shrubbery.

ARAKAWA: [Laughs] I myself find that surprising. Shall we take a walk around it?

ROBERT: Go around it? Why bother? I can see everything I need to from here.

GINS: Isn't it wonderful that you can see all of it at once—as if you were looking at it in plan?

ANGELA: That would make this pile of junk a very bumpy blueprint.

GINS: Let's take ourselves around to the other side.

ROBERT: Sure.

GINS: Having made our way around the house, we are now on its south side.

ROBERT: How about that! A huge stack of clothes has been thrown together. Assembled randomly? But the way it's piled up here on this side seems to be identical to how it has been stacked up over there at the northern end of the heap. Heights and depths differ, though.

ANGELA: We were simply unable to discern the symmetry from the other side. It was only once we had moved around it that . . . Our being able to make out so much more from this vantage point, do we chalk that up to how the light is hitting it on this side, to what a northern light brings to the fore?

ROBERT: Could it be that the intricate way things are piled on the left side—the west, I guess—closely resembles the pile or piles giving it its shape on the right—the east? I am actually beginning to spot some defined edges here and there.

GINS: In which case I say we go in now. Do you want to go back around to the north side, or shall we enter from here?

ROBERT: Diagonally opposite us . . . Is that an ordinary house over there?

ARAKAWA: That's a tract house from the fifties.

ROBERT: Where we are standing strikes me as somehow an extension of that house's front yard.

GINS: Why don't we go back around this house to enter it through its front door.

ANGELA: This—this whatever it is—has a front and a back?

GINS: Of course.

ROBERT: A front door by which to enter this doormat sort of thing, this giant shower cap . . .

GINS: Here we are. Try to get in from, let me see, about here. You need to come back a few inches.

ANGELA: How do you expect me to get into something this totally flat to the ground?

GINS: You have to go under it. Pick it up and insert yourself into it.

ROBERT: I can't get a hold of it. There's nothing to hold onto.

ANGELA: Wow, it's so light! What material is this?

GINS: A new material developed by NASA.

ANGELA: Is it fireproof?

ARAKAWA: Definitely, and waterproof. It's flexible, durable, and, to our delight, it happens to provide great insulation as well.

ANGELA: That's unbelievable.

GINS: Take that section of material you are holding in your left hand and push it up a little higher. Bring it up to at least waist level.

ANGELA: Oh, here's something that looks like a handle. If I hold onto it to slide the material . . .

ARAKAWA: You need to slide it to the left at the same time you push it upwards.

ANGELA: Yes, it opened. This is scary. It keeps changing . . . volumes open with my every motion . . . With each push . . . it's changing right in front of my eyes, with each push . . . pushing open . . . opening. How I spread my arms to push it open . . . It takes shape from how . . . If I push it to one side . . . It is as if I am that snail . . . How does that song go again?

GINS: I have no trouble recalling that song whose lyrics are the parent text to this house's theme song. It goes like this:

Snails

But getting out of tight ground is quite another matter.
The more credit to them for going in,
given how much harder it is to get out.

Loving clumped earth, snails *go* along glued bodily to it.
They carry it with them, they eat it, they excrete it.
They *go* through it. It *goes* through them.

An interpenetration in the best possible taste
because, as it were, of complementary tones:
passive and active elements. The one simultaneously
bathes and feeds the other,
which covers ground at the same time that it eats.
The moment it displays its nudity,
reveals its vulnerable form,
its modesty compels it to move on.
No sooner does it expose itself than it's on the go.

Note too that you cannot conceive of a snail
emerging from its shell and not moving.
The moment it stops to rest
it pulls back into its shell.

(Other things might be mentioned about snails. To begin
with, their characteristic humidity. Their *sang froid.* Their extensibility.)

Snails *go* along glued bodily to first and second shells.
Clumped earth: second shell.
They carry it with them, they eat it, they excrete it.
They *go* through it. It *goes* through them.*

---

*Both the theme song and its parent text use in full Francis Ponge's poem "Escar-
gots." Ponge's snail musings adumbrate our concept of an architectural body. Did
the poet go toward the snail, we wonder, with a similar concept in hand? Or—
and this is more likely, given Ponge's express wish to be at all costs fair-minded,
that is, to take the side of things and creatures—did the gastropods simply present this to him, to a mammalian explorer, as a reward for his reportorial efforts
on their behalf. In any case, there can be no doubt that, as great and as intimate

ROBERT: That's heartening. I begin to see what is expected of us in here. First off, we need to stretch our limbs as much as possible. When I stretch my arms up as if I am about to hit a volleyball, the material rides up and . . . I can see a fairly large area. Is that a kitchen facility . . . a kitchen in the center?

GINS: Yes, that is the kitchen. Your arms are raised up high. Atlas supporting the globe. And do you see where that gets you—it gets you a house that begins to have rooms.

ANGELA: Rooms form depending on how we move. If I bend down, I nearly lose the room. Would you open up the room a little more where you are?

ROBERT: I will play a caryatid and you go off to the farthest end. I am beginning to feel more at ease within this. I find it much less strange. But, the thing is, the three of you now appear to me as a bit on the strange side. Are you emitting snail pheromones or something?

GINS: You're at least four inches taller than the rest of us . . . so you probably should be the one to hold up the structure near the small hill by the window.

ROBERT: Wow! It really opens up into a large area, despite its having an incredibly low ceiling. Lights come on as areas open.

ANGELA: The floor is uneven. Does it slope?

GINS: For a closer look at our effect on this house, let us each

---

as the human architectural heritage is, the architectural heritage of snails is as great and far more intimate. That the architectural know-how of this gastropod prefigures the concept of an architectural body, a concept that, for us, has been decades in the making, has as stark a reality for us as—now, little snail, cover your ears for a moment—the stabbing of an undersized fork into the body of an escargot, the plunking of it into one's mouth, and a biting into and a toothing through a muscularity god-awfully reminiscent of tongue. Francis Ponge, "Escargots," *Selected Poems,* translated by Margaret Gutton, John Montague, and C. K. Williams, edited by Margaret Gutton (Winston-Salem, N.C.: Wake Forest University Press, 1997), 38.

take a deep breath. The material expands and contracts as
we do.

ROBERT: Where do people sleep? Or take showers? What
about cooking?

Everything that can be done in an ordinary house can be
done in this one, but some maneuvering may be necessary to
reach the point of sitting pretty. Each piece of material on the
pile has ribs or spokes that open like those of an umbrella.
Ready-to-be-activated expanding mechanisms lie at four-foot
intervals. Depending on which setting has been selected, the
house lies low, just as it was when you first saw it, and as it
has remained all the while you've been in here, or it expands a
little, getting some height, or, on the highest setting, it really
achieves its full stature, including a dome and a vaulted ceiling. There's a setting to accommodate anything you want to
do in the house. For example, you had asked before about how
feasible it was to light a stove and do some cooking. Cooking
can take place within an ample kitchen that forms and stays
formed until one selects a lower setting that causes the material to close back in and down. We predict that drawing the
unfurled material back and down to be within touching distance will be a high priority for most inhabitants of houses like
this. Remote-control switches operate sensors that bloom and
fabricate the house on behalf of those who are ill or handi-
capped. You are not given a finished house but instead form it
through your movements and through those of whoever else
is in there with you. All materials are impervious to weather.

Four people have entered a work of architecture that floats
the Sited Awareness Hypothesis—or, as it is also known, the
Architectural Body Hypothesis (see chapter 5). Upon being
entered and used, this work of architecture, which only be-

comes what it is through being entered and used, gives corroborating evidence for this hypothesis. Architecture as hypothesis plays off of the long-short history of architecture as non-hypothesis. Constructed to exist in the tense of *what if,* it presents itself as intentionally provisional, replacing definite form with tentative form, the notion of a lasting structure with that of an adaptive one.

∞

GINS: Yes, cooking—that doesn't present a problem. The house has a full complement of rooms. Whatever people do in other houses, they can do in this.

ROBERT: You mean people can actually live here?

GINS: Of course. I was hoping you'd want to.

ARAKAWA: Live here and do daily research.

ROBERT: Research into what?

ARAKAWA: Into what goes into being a person. This place can help you do that. What part of the house do you think you're in now?

ANGELA: I haven't the foggiest idea. But I at least have it in me now to feel it to be one room or another. I'm interested in doing that research you speak of.

GINS: We've entered the living room. We probably should sit down and rest for awhile, so let's head for the couch and chairs.

ROBERT: Oh, really?

GINS: Since the living room remains missing, we will have to stretch out and reach up to form it. Have you ever pitched a tent?

ROBERT: Not one this large. I have some nice memories of watching a crew put up a huge tent for a friend's wedding . . . and then of being inside it.

GINS: Let's see. There are four of us, so that means we have

four poles available. Of course, on a higher setting the structure could rally many more poles . . . as many as needed.

ROBERT: But if I am going to be a tent pole or caryatid, how
can I also sit in a chair?

ARAKAWA: If we initiate the form, other spines within the surrounding material will kick in and take over . . . for ten min-
utes at a time.

GINS: Of course, it would really get going and open up if we
had the house on one of its higher settings—one that engages
the whole set of spine-deploying mechanisms embedded in
the fabric.

ANGELA: How many settings does this living space have?

GINS: Three. A zero setting that we call the *snail setting*. And
then a medium setting, in which the material stays always at
a slight remove from those within it; we have named this the
close-to-snail setting. The highest setting is the one that does it
all; when this is on, spine-deploying mechanisms are fully engaged; we have named it *roomy*.

ROBERT: At this moment . . . you have it on the snail setting,
I think it would be fair to say. All the while . . . always turned
to that?

ARAKAWA: Snail setting all along. This setting provides the
most intense way to use this . . . tool . . . this piece of equipment. This house is a tool, a procedural one.

GINS: A functional tool, whether it be a hammer, a telephone,
or a telescope, extends the senses, but a procedural tool examines and reorders the sensorium.

ARAKAWA: Let us then cloak ourselves in solemnly merry
stanzas that guide us in the use of this piece of equipment
within which we are moving.

Humansnails

But getting out of tight spots is quite another matter.
The more credit to them for picking up an edge and going in,
given how much harder it is to get out.

Loving *their* medium, humansnails *go* along glued bodily
to it,
all their breathing closing in palpably around them.
They carry this with them, they swallow it,
they expel, exude, and disperse it.
They *go* through it. It *goes* through them.

Their medium: sited awareness
All that a humansnail disperses: (its) ubiquitous site.
Call all that a humansnail disperses: (its) architectural body.
An interpenetration in the best possible taste
because, as it were, of complementary tones:
passive and active elements. The one simultaneously
bathes and feeds the other,
which covers the distance it breathes in and out and forms.

Humansnails *go* along glued bodily to second skins or shells
(architectural surrounds).
First shells: shaped volumes of the beloved medium of humansnails.
First shells: shaped volumes that form by virtue of actions humansnails take within second shells (architectural surrounds).
First shells: relatively large atmospheric globular samples of the
beloved medium—medium as oneself??—that wraps around
humansnails.
First shell: on-the-spot humansnail-made wrappings of sited
awareness.
Have the man-made become as to the point as the snail-made.

Thick with one's own breathing.
Thick with one's own landing-site configurations.
They carry landing sites with them, they swallow them,
heuristically for a direct mapping.
They expel, exude, and disperse landing-site configurations.
They *go* through their ubiquitous sites,

i.e., the sum of all landing sites of each moment.
Their ubiquitous sites *go* through them.

Note too that you cannot conceive of a humansnail
emerging from its shells and not moving.
The moment it stops to rest
it pulls back into its next pair of shells.

(Other things might be mentioned about humansnails. To begin with, their characteristic timidity. Their *sang froid.* Their
extensibility.)

A person's landing-site dispersal usually does not straightfor-
wardly present itself as "breathing material." How dare we put
scare quotes around the breathable massenergy of the universe
turned world?! Oh to have the opportunities of a snail!! Would
that you could check up on what disperses under your aus-
pices as what you feel yourself to be. Your actions cling to you
and respond to you as if they were growing out of you like
fingernails. Your house becomes your pet or you become the
pet of your house, or a mixture of the two.

ANGELA: It's time for us to move through it now, isn't it?
ARAKAWA: It sure is. I'm bringing my hands down to my sides
and bending slightly forward and just plunging ahead. Each
of you should assume a similar posture and then forge ahead.
Each goes off in a different direction.
ROBERT: When do we get out of the snail phase?
GINS: Well, you know, it's possible to dwell in this house for
days on end without ever moving it off the snail setting. I

think for this, your first time in it, we should probably leave the dial where it is. It's the most direct way we know to re-order sensateness . . . sensitivity . . . sensibility . . . one's sensorium . . . landing-site dispersal . . . sited awareness.

ANGELA: As a way to engineer that direct mapping the two of you speak of? If so, what should we do? Should we move around more?

ARAKAWA: With less to attend to in this snail-setting living room than in ordinary ones, it becomes easier to focus in on the effect each action has. Come toward me, toward this couch, moving in an exaggeratedly slow way. Can you see it from where you are?

ROBERT: I see no couch. I can't even see you at this point.

ARAKAWA: Then move toward the sound of my voice. Go a little slower.

ROBERT: I have spotted a couch leg.

GINS: Head toward it—still in slow motion—and, as you do, describe everything you see and feel.

ROBERT: Something that extends from the back of my head all the way down along the broad of my back to a little below my waist pushes me forward. And with every step, I feel and see a bobbing horizon, a low one, a horizon that I look down to actually. As I carefully dole out the movements that constitute this step I am taking, using tiny haulings-up and miniscule pushings-through to lift my right leg, I see being added to a room—a room?—that moments before had within it only a single couch leg, what I make out to be your foot, and Angela's frame from her shoulders on down. Angela, I cannot believe how much you are swaying.

ARAKAWA: That little group you describe equals your ubiquitous site, everywhere you have landed or could land. Call all that which is in the immediate vicinity of a person a ubiquitous site.

GINS: This is a ubiquity of *you* . . . inclusive of . . . your power to compose a world and be in contact with it . . . inclusive of all contact, of whatever variety, you have with the world.

ARAKAWA: Defined to let loose an everywhere at once, the word *ubiquitous* even so fails to convey this covering of everywhere at once we experience in here. The rapid succession of events called experience overreaches ubiquity, I guess.

GINS: The number of purposeful actions required of you has been suddenly greatly reduced. It becomes easier to observe yourself as an agent of action because this closed-in world exacts fewer purposive moves.

ARAKAWA: Even so, there is still a semblance of an agent and there is still a great scattering.

GINS: Yes, it becomes predominantly a world of landing sites. Down to that level of abstraction.

ARAKAWA: Each of us becomes an everywhere evenly distributed agent, dropping the centralizing habit that members of our species have had for such a terribly long time. What I am about to say might sound irrational to you—but if it turns out to be what is going on, then rationality will have to be redefined. An everywhere evenly distributed agent—a ubiquitous site or an architectural body—will even be able to renegotiate gravity.

GINS: The gravity that gets accorded to apportioning out, which, for a more complete picture, probably ought to be spoken of as an apportioning out and in.

ROBERT: It feels as if the material will go from only clinging to my back to fully engulfing me. With each thrusting of my limbs, or head and neck, or torso against the house that sits on top of me and drapes over me, I find myself in drastically changed circumstances.

ARAKAWA: When in the snail setting, the house only has rooms that the actions taken within it produce.

GINS: You are casting about as you always do, but with a difference. In the snail setting, the feel of the house and its weight cast you even before you can start casting about on your own. Through its casting of you, through its determining of how you come to be kinesthetically and proprioceptively disposed, the house prompts your actions. How we have been cast, how we are kinesthetically disposed, determines how we choose to act and if we can.

ARAKAWA: Closing in on you, the tactile surroundings sculpt kinesthetic possibility or kinesthetic with-it-ness. This sculpted kinesthetic with-it-ness—the tentativeness of any moment—can be thought of as the matrix of person.

GINS: Kinesthesia—body feel or bodily feeling—can never be had apart from imaging. To begin with, to move at all . . . One needs to image, for example, where to place one's arm prior to moving it.

ANGELA: Everything is responsive to my every move. I am at the wide-open part of an enclosure shaped like a side pocket of a pair of slacks. The draping material extends out from my neck and shoulders down toward the pocket's narrow end. This end is not sewn in place but is instead a temporary horizon, bobbing, all activated by . . . my every move.

ROBERT: Being within this enclosure makes landing more palpable.

ANGELA: As far as landing goes: the material lands on me, upon me. Through its actions, my body "lands punches" on the material. The activated bobbing-up-and-down horizon that is draped into shifting place lands ever differently. A lot depends on whether I land on my feet or not.

GINS: I must say that what we have enclosed in here, within, as you aptly describe it, a shallow pocket, is "that which registers."

ARAKAWA: The body has a spherical kinesthetic-proprioceptive-tactile dispersive potential, tentativeness at the ready.

GINS: There is that which can register whatever turns up . . . The registerings are the landing sites we speak of.

ARAKAWA: We would like to be able to keep track of all that gets registered at any given moment. That within this pocket one has far fewer than the usual number of things and events to take note of suits our purpose well.

ROBERT: Fewer things to keep track of in the outside world, but as far as the body is concerned nothing changes: the number of places in the body that need at each moment to be kept track of stays roughly the same, doesn't it?

ARAKAWA: Yes and no. The number of landing sites particular to the body itself stays within a predictable range, which happens to be a fairly wide one. But with the house on the snail setting, the number of strictly bodily landing sites cluster at the high end of that range.

GINS: In addition to standing stock still, close your eyes for a moment. What do you find as your body?

ROBERT: I find my body to be at the mercy of this material that doesn't leave it alone. Always lightly resting on my back and responsive to my every move, this thing you call a house threatens to . . .

GINS: At how many spots along your back would you say you feel it? You know, any registering of a point of physical contact equals a tactile landing site.

ARAKAWA: If the contact feels continuous, then you have probably joined several smaller tactile landing sites into a few large ones. Your head, neck, shoulders, back: a single landing site or two.

GINS: It might be a good idea to try to re-divide them, that is, to approximate how they might have been before they were combined. Tactile landing sites report: that is there. Coupled with kinesthetic landing sites and imaging landing sites they report: that is there as that.

ROBERT: It is as if I had been turned into a statue of myself . . . not the caryatid of before. From the points of contact— tactile landing sites, I guess—forward I am entering into, or feeling into, the feel of my tissues. Ubiquitous tissues feel to me to be very breath-like but simultaneously not that breath-like.

GINS: Kinesthetic landing sites are of course closely allied with tactile landing ones. Often tactile landing sites will prompt kinesthetic ones to come alive. Because you are being so tactilely activated from behind, your kinesthetic-proprioceptive wherewithal is now being cast with a decidedly frontal orientation. Tactility and kinesthesia toggle-switch into one another, so, were you to suddenly happen to bring your hand to your chest, kinesthesia would immediately give way to tactility at that spot.

ROBERT: About kinesthesia . . . I feel all porous and it, kinesthesia, functions as that which animates porosity. I am a filter, and this shallow pocket we are within is another, a different type of filter, perhaps a slightly more porous one. Rapid exchanges are going on between these two filters, and the speed and quality of the exchange depends on how my body . . . My body casts about within this material and then actions and events cast my body. A lot depends on how that sculpture, my cast body of felt sense, goes on to cast the rest of the pocket's volume.

ARAKAWA: Because your eyes have been closed, it would seem that what you have described has been imaged. But as all description springs into action within kinesthetic-proprioceptive bounds, your visualizing of your body with your eyes closed has surely been produced by perceptual as well as imaging landing sites. This ought not to come as a surprise to anyone; but nearly everyone finds this to be surprising. Open your eyes.

ROBERT: Wow!! It's all so different. But I remained motionless, as you instructed me to, and so, I believe, did the rest of you. It could not have been only our breathing that so greatly altered this place.

GINS: And yet . . . to the extent that breathing is sufficient to change landing site configuration . . . As abstractions that act as conduits for apportioning out, landing sites . . . Or landing sites may be abstractions, but they are ones designed to let that which gets apportioned out, that which is prior to abstracting, flow through with the minimal amount of interference. What, I should ask you, is landing for you now?

ANGELA: The entire house is landing on me . . . on us. There are so many landings I hardly know where to begin.

ROBERT: When I breathe in there are a lot of landings as a result of that . . . I am feeling my breathing more than I ever have before. What I breathe in lands in the lungs . . . but I can't exactly track it to there, although in a way I can. But my attending to all this breathing . . . my solicitousness to my own breathing, would you characterize all that taken together as landing?

ARAKAWA: Yes, I think so. I am thrilled that you came up with that. Linking breathing and landing . . . we hadn't quite gotten to that yet.

ANGELA: What a cozy spot. If you don't mind, I think I will curl up right here and take a nap.

4
Architectural Surround

Let our species cease being stunned into silence and passivity, into defeatism, by a formal architecture that seems so accomplished but that leads nowhere. Members of our species have been stunned into passivity by what should be their greatest ally. To counter the deer-in-the-headlights effect, we have turned from speaking of architecture, vast architecture, to speaking of what of vast architecture a person can encompass in any given moment, naming this the architectural surround. This is architecture at the ready, at everyone's disposal. It is not monumentality but an approachable workaday architecture our species is in need of.

An architectural surround's features: its boundaries and all objects and persons within it. Each circumjacency has a characteristic set of features. Here are some architectural surrounds and their characteristic sets of features. In the case of an architectural surround that is nothing more than a small enclosure in a wheat field formed by many stalks having been trampled upon, the set includes a floor of trampled-upon wheat stalks, walls consisting of wheat stalks, bent stragglers mixed in with intact ones, and sky for a ceiling. The set of features for a kitchen will be all that makes it a kitchen, including the woman putting a roast in the oven. The set of characteristic features for an immensely large architectural surround such as a city will be everything that makes it a city, including all those bustling or ambling through it.

Similarly to how she flexes her muscles, a person flexes her surroundings—both are with her and of her always. Landing-site dispersal and a flexing of the circumambient determine and describe the world that lies within one's ambit of the moment. A person who is noting what is around her is dispersing landing sites; as body-wide landing-site dispersal registers the body's immersion within a volume held in place by certain demarcations, recording particulars about boundaries, a person will feel herself surrounded first according to one description of the world, then another. Moving within an architectural surround, a person fashions an evolving matrix, an architectural surround not entirely of her own making. Repeatedly, incessantly, a person surrounds herself by conforming in a particular set of ways to what surrounds her. Constrained by her environment, she proceeds to piece together an architectural surround that maps onto the one within which she finds herself. In a glance, she takes in a tree, a lake, or a wall. Glancing in that direction again, but this time having lifted, for example, her right leg to start walking toward X, she . . .

∞

Questions that query the degree to which persons are surroundings-bound need to be posed by actually erecting measuring frames around them. If persons can never be extricated from surroundings, then what must be looked at is the extent to which they are bound to and influenced by them. In what respects and how variegatedly do physical surroundings invite bodily action? How far out into the environment does an organism that persons extend? To what extent do surroundings influence thoughts and actions?

A rounding of multiple foci into a supposed whole occurs again and again, continually. One such surrounding of oneself follows upon the last, and there comes to be a layering of surroundings, a summing up of surroundings, into the singular plural of "the surroundings." So much happens all at once, and *surrounding* and *to be surrounded* are spatiotemporally multilayered, this plural oneness ("the surroundings") lets you know. The words *confines* and *bounds* deliver the same message of a multiplicity of events, the active everything through which one moves—from a supposedly single viewpoint. These terms are conveniently all-inclusive; the word *surroundings* in one of its uses designates the people in one's vicinity or members of an entourage.

Preexisting those who enter them, architectural surrounds stand as elaborately structured pretexts for action. Ready and waiting to be entered, even when in disarray, they are always-encountered and often-noticed but little-understood atmospheric conditioners. Someone might make a convincing case for doubting that she exists or that isolated objects do, but it would be preposterous for her to try to use doubt to wipe away features and elements of an entire architectural surround. It would be unusual and unlikely for someone holding a glass beneath an open faucet and filling it with water to doubt the existence of either any part of this situation or of the situation as a whole. The question "Is this real or an illusion?" would seem not to be an option at such a moment. This whole situation—the sink, faucet, running stream of water, glass, hand, kitchen floor, wall-tiles, and windows, for a start—is of her sensorium within which she pours all liquids and drinks them up, but it is also constructed in place and is as such a place she can enter and with which she can link up in all manner of ways. All organisms-persons work hard, but none could work that hard, that is, no one could pull off the creation of an entire kitchen with water-producing faucet without prods, prompts, and props—that is, without the help of that set of features characteristic of this appliance-filled architectural surround. It would also be ridiculous for someone using a flashlight to find the path out of a labyrinthine cave and bumping up against uneven walls and low overhangs or tripping upon rocks and stalagmites and then sliding into and splashing through shallow puddles to wonder if indeed this might be a hollowed-out figment of her imagination.

One's living room is and isn't one's own sensorium. All that is tentative is in the realm of sensoria; all that appears to be definite has been physically constructed.

The living room one enters maps directly onto one's tentativeness as to what it might turn out to be, that is, onto one's budding suppositions as to what might be holding in place as this the living room. One's sporadic linkings with features of an architectural surround thread a defined enterable, hollowed-out volume throughout and into the midst of the pulsed arraying of possibilities to be pursued. Because any landing upon something, any type of contact, will, by turning a hesitant placing into something more definite, reduce tentativeness or put it on hold, it is a fairly easy matter to design an architectural surround that will direct and channel tentativeness.

∞

An ordinary room: a classic example of an architectural surround. Architectural surrounds exist only in relation to those moving within them. Consider a living room in relation to those using it. Recognizable as the type of room it is, but never read the same way twice, a standard living room exists as an enclosing framework, each set of walls, and each wall individually, and surely the floor, too, a backdrop that can frame action. Although for a person on the move, room size and shape will fluctuate greatly, they will not appear to. Each person knows without doubt the size of her own living room. Within this opened up and insisted upon hollowed-out volume that she calls "my living room," a person initiates tentatives, composes actions, shifting her bodily frame accordingly, taking the room with her, that is, taking it up differently depending on how she winds up being positioned. Standard rooms evoke a relatively predictable set of actions. In the good fit of a familiar room, one feels as if the tentativeness underlying actions has been molded. Even someone moving through an apartment with a plan of it in hand does not, because she selects her surroundings and assembles them as she goes, succeed in capturing the whole of it. Architectural surrounds stand as shaping molds for the *What happens next?* of life.

∞

Putting only a single artifact into an environment will—if someone is around to happen onto the scene—turn it into an architectural surround.

Having once begun to architect their surroundings, human beings never stop. A person turns a desert or a forest into an architectural surround by how she moves through it. Advancing and cutting paths, fending for herself and defending herself, she uses her limbs to erect enclosures or break them. That which has been architected blocks, guides, facilitates, comforts, contains, or suggests containing.

An architecturally imbued person will architect every manner of surroundings. An architecturally imbued person will architect every manner of surroundings, even a vast open plain. Any architectural surround she once experienced can become a four-dimensional point of reference for a person standing on an open plain.

Organisms that person need to *construct* their hypotheses and enter them, surrounding themselves with ordered presentations of their suppositions. Our claim: architecture can help a person figure herself out.

∞

Environment-organism-person is all that is the case. Isolating persons from their architectural surrounds leads to a dualism no less pernicious than that of mind and body.

∞

Architectural surrounds that are not specifically set up to be procedural hardly address tentativeness at all. Until now, prior to the existence of a truly procedural architecture, the atmospheric conditioning that architectural surrounds have performed on sensoria has been relatively routine, addressed to and revolving around basic bodily needs. But even the most surefooted, self-confident person brings hesitancy in abundance to her relationship with an architectural surround, for part of being a person is to feel uncertain in regard to and tentative about what comes next. Tentativeness, which produces out of its own generative chaos the possibility of a firm or definite sense of things, needs to receive directions.

Contribute your room, your architectural surround of the moment, to this text. For your room to be of use in what follows, it needs to be transformed into a work of procedural architecture. Note where in the room you are and the direction in which you are facing. To have this room—the room in which you happen to be reading this—stand out distinctly as the room it is, select and keep vivid a representative group of its features. Now take the room and give its floor a ten-degree tilt along its longest length (if the room is square, either side is fine). Make a double of your room thus tilted and place it next to the original. Seesaw the floor of the double so that it ends up tilting in the opposite direction.

ARCHITECT: We have now been in both rooms. It is apparent that the two together frame the impact on us of an architectural surround, that is, of the room in which you are reading this text.
READER: I lean differently into the situation of exactly this room within each of its exemplars.

ARCHITECT: Perfect.

READER: The characteristic features completely match of course from one room to the other—except, that is, for how they land in me.

ARCHITECT: Kinesthetically, these twins, as we heed the slants, present themselves as complementary opposites.

READER: Why the tilt?

ARCHITECT: To catch an architectural surround. To catch the catching (fielding) of an architectural surround. All of it all at once. To know one's room like the back of one's hand: to register one's landing-site dispersal in its entirety.

READER: And without the two opposing tilts?

ARCHITECT: That doubling also would work to bring the architectural surround of the moment sharply into focus. But we would no longer be able to observe and study exactly what—were all else equal, all other landing sites being equal—the effect would be on thought and behavior of two oppositely dispersed (tilted) sequencings of kinesthetic-landing-site configurations.

READER: Yes, and our organism-given tentativeness. It would be snapped up into definiteness, I guess, by the room we know so definitively. A much too hasty resolving of the indeterminate into the "known."

ARCHITECT: To slow down the automatic dispersal. To enter the dispersing itself?

READER: A hesitancy permeates the world in its abundance.

ARCHITECT: Not to get too completely absorbed or sucked up into the process of landing upon . . .

∞

Against the environment of the new territory that is her extended I, a person throws tentatives that land as functions and schemata, most of which join up with her, becoming of her by reprogramming her. Although the organism-person has the potential to become a person, it does not necessarily become one, or remain one. Everything begins for these organisms with *a tentative constructing toward a holding in place.* The environmental communal, which has everything to do with how an organism persons, can, when reworked in a concerted manner, lead to persons being able to supersede themselves.

5
Procedural Architecture

What Counts as Architecture? What Counts as Biosleave? What Counts as Architectural Body?

Start by thinking of architecture as *a tentative constructing toward a holding in place.* Architecture's holding in place occurs within and as part of a prevailing atmospheric condition that others routinely call *biosphere* but which we, feeling the need to stress its dynamic nature, have renamed *bioscleave.*

All species belonging to bioscleave exist only tentatively (which remains true whatever turns out to be the truth about natural selection, whether it happens randomly or with directionality), with some species, all things being unequal, existing on a far more tentative basis than others. Additionally, bioscleave stays breathable and in the picture only so long as elements take hold of each other in particular ways, only so long as there can be a cleaving of a this to a that and a cleaving of a this off of a that. So that there might be new and different link-ups, fresh points of departure, ever renewed *tentative constructing toward a holding in place,* a firm and definite taking hold, which gives one sense of the term to cleave, must also readily entail cutting apart, cut-off, relinquishment, the other sense of the term. Should a crucial element fail to hold its own, bioscleave would go missing, collapsing into untempered atmosphere, leaving (but no one would be there to tell) an uninhabitable planet in its wake. A single missing element (carbon or oxygen) or an aberrant formation of a molecule, to say nothing of a large-scale cataclysmic event, could make bioscleave vanish, bringing an abrupt end to millennia of *tentative constructing toward a holding in place.* In studying so tenuous and elusive an event-fabric as bioscleave, the making of cut-and-dried separations, such as distinguishing between subject and object, should be avoided.

Because bioscleave itself occurs as a demonstrably *tentative constructing toward a holding in place,* architectural works constructed into it cannot be anything but tentative; furthermore—and it is for this reason that we have chosen tentativeness as an organizing principle in our practice—it is not enough to know that in deep time all architectural works are fleeting things: it is necessary to construct architectural works that reflect bioscleave's intrinsic tentativeness. An architectural work that will serve the body well will maximize its chances of drawing on and blending with bioscleave, positioning the body in such a way that it can best coordinate itself within its surroundings. Simply, pretending that architecture is not tentative is just that, only a pretense. Architecture will come into its own when it becomes thoroughly associated and aligned with the body, that active other *tentative constructing toward a holding in place,* the ever-on-the-move body. The tense of architecture should be not that of "This is this" or "Here is this" but instead that of "What's going on?"

Staying current with bioscleave, remaining alive as part of it, involves keeping pace with the tentativeness it brings to bear, staying focused on the elusiveness as such of this tenuous event-fabric or event-matrix. Everything is tentative, but some things or events have a tentativeness with a faster-running clock than others. So that there can at least be a keeping pace with bioscleave's tentativeness, it becomes necessary to divine how best to join events into an event-fabric, which surely involves learning to vary the speed at which one fabricates *tentative constructings toward holding in place.*

Architecture occurs as one of many ways life sees fit to conduct and construct itself, a form of life, and all forms of life have, without doubt, as of this date, but a limited and uncertain existence. Even so, thus far only nomads have held architecture to be as a matter of course tentative.

Life—Bios—would seem to be constituted by interactions between *tentative constructings toward a holding in place,* with the body, the body-in-action, surely the main fiddler at the fair. Bodily movements that take place within and happen in relation to works of architecture, architectural surrounds, are to some extent formative of them. Those living within and reading and making what they can of an architectural surround are instrumental in and crucial to its *tentative constructing toward a holding in place.* We do not mean to suggest that architecture exists only for the one who beholds or inhabits it, but rather that the body-in-action and the architectural surround should not be defined apart from each other, or apart from bioscleave. Architectural works can direct the body's *tentative constructing toward a holding in place,* its forming in place. But it is also the case that how the body moves determines what turns out to hold together as architecture for it.

What is authoritative in human life: a person's tentativeness—a totally constructed tentativeness—surefooted rightful hesitation, on-the-hesitating-mark. Persons need to be rescued from self-certainty, but they also need to put their tentativeness in precise order in relation to works of architecture. The hypotheses of procedural architecture query how it is possible— what *a tentative constructing toward a holding in place* entails— to be a knowing body in a bioscleave—the ins and outs of viability.

> What stems from the body, by way of awareness, should be held
> to be of it. Any site at which a person finds an X to exist should
> be considered a contributing segment of her awareness.
>   Architectural Body Hypothesis/Sited Awareness Hypothesis

This supposition would seem to state the obvious were it not for the fact that the historical record reveals awareness to have rarely, if ever, been defined as sited, or studied as such. Recognize, this supposition urges, that awareness sites itself all over the place at once; or better, that a person positions herself within her surroundings by taking her surroundings up as her sited awareness. Sites of sited awareness are, of course, landing sites of the moment. Put in evidence in this hypothesis is the disparity that exists between the world as it happens—awareness as indeed sited—and the world, reduced and distorted, made to appear as other than what it happens as—awareness abstracted out of any surroundings.

Putting two seemingly discrete *tentative constructings towards a holding in place* forward as one, the Architectural Body Hypothesis/Sited Awareness Hypothesis, a supposition that guides procedural architecture, would have it that a person never be considered apart from her surroundings. It announces the indivisibility of seemingly separable fields of bioscleave: a person and an architectural surround. The two together give procedural architecture its basic unit of study, the architectural body. The Architectural Body Hypothesis/Sited Awareness Hypothesis puts forward the idea that embodied mind, a current way of referring to mind or awareness so as to give body its due, extends out beyond the body-proper into the architectural surround; the surrounding bioscleave needs to be weighed in as part of awareness's body. This hypothesis would have us never forget that we are babies of bioscleave and are therefore only comprehensible (to ourselves) in terms of it.

What Counts as Procedural?

Bioscleave—people breathe it, it sustains them—has parts and elements, many of which exhibit an order, even as it presents itself as an enormously confused mass with operative factors that cannot be distinguished. Who moves through this mass of chaos, this massive mix of order and chaos, has sited awareness buried there within it. People are forced to abstract in order to proceed, but any abstracting requires that not as much be taken into consideration as ought to be. A person can never get to the bottom of her own alertness. Having to abstract in order to proceed, an organism that persons is half-abstracted from the start. She behaves as if she were on her own recognizance, never quite sure that it is valid to assume this. People get drawn off in this direction or that. In a world of persistent inexplicability, everyone will be fairly direction-less, even those appearing to have chosen a definite course of action. The world as one finds it: a concatenation of partial procedures or procedure-like occurrences, diffuse or defused procedures, incomplete or bedeviling ones.

Calculated measures that have distinct and purposeful steps do take shape under the aegis of some agency. But because what (if anything) authorizes agency within bioscleave lies hidden, agency, all agency, remains suspect. Defining procedure as a process that is the work of an agent, or that at least implies agency, we attempt to smoke out hidden agents or agency or to grow (the basis for) new ones.

People interact with bioscleave largely through what has come to be called *procedural knowing,* a term covering both instinctual sequences and encoded knowing, that is, habitual patterns of activity. Perceiving, walking, talking, and eating, for example, happen as procedural knowing. Acquiring a skill involves integrating all steps needed for skillfully performing a task and then reducing them to a procedure. Whatever has come to be know-how has been cast as procedural; the many activities and considerations that subsist as procedural know-ing within or to one side of sited awareness, taking up fewer of its sites now than they had need of before they were thus reduced, free it to be active elsewhere. With steps and nuances of coordinating skills handled apart from awareness, a person can go on to acquire still other coordinating skills. The instinctual and the newly ingrained get played back through operations lying outside awareness—as procedurally triggered occurrences. Learned behavior equals procedures that can automatically, minus awareness, be set in motion. Steps are performed outside awareness.

Landing-site dispersal, that which transpires as sited awareness, is coordinated beneath awareness. If thinking is thought of as a subroutine of this siting procedure, it too must be regarded as procedural. Even thinking as traditionally defined— that is, thinking taken as a single course of action, which, we suggest, is an outrageously reductive definition—would seem to depend on procedures. In any case, when sets of instructions are carried out and tasks performed, one is tempted to speak of procedure; shall we categorize thinking as a body-wide, no, bioscleave-wide, mixture of procedures belonging to different realms, a thus far ineffable and unexplainable series of procedurally conducted occurrences?

Procedures do and do not walk up to one to introduce themselves as existing. Processes linked, no matter how briefly, to awareness: procedures, procedural. Rather than flat-out knowing, there is a continual anticipating, self-guarding, accommodating, allowing, bypassing—all of which can be counted as procedural. All bodily dynamics: procedurally orchestrated. The unconscious: the procedural. Innate functions, defense mechanisms, built-in and built-up tendencies, hidden knowing: procedures at the behest of someone or something—procedures born of procedures?

That which counts as procedural will need to be enlarged and made to exist so that it can be entered wittingly. Only once the procedural can on its own account be entered, only once the procedural has been writ large, will members of our species have it in them to complete centuries-old procedures that, having remained unfinished, have left them in the lurch, bereft and doubly bereft. A constructed world that has, with great forethought, been tactically posed and thus been given its procedural due will instruct people in brand-new coordinating skills and in the compounding of skills attained. Ability to coordinate a greater number of skills leads to a freer and wider-ranging and more perspicacious intellect.

∞

This brings us to the second of the three hypotheses underpinning procedural architecture:

> It is because we are creatures of an insufficiently procedural bioscleave that the human lot remains untenable.
>   Insufficiently Procedural Bioscleave Hypothesis

Within an insufficiently procedural bioscleave, members of the human species have neither the wherewithal to figure out the nature of their agency nor the requisite skill to engineer for themselves what would amount to a reversible destiny. Although it has plenty of processes and procedures in place, bioscleave consistently lets us down, that is, drops us one by one—we are mortal—because procedures through which we could sustain ourselves indefinitely are lacking to it.

The Insufficiently Procedural Bioscleave Hypothesis does not give the universe and its bioscleave a failing grade, only an incomplete.

Those who are of bioscleave need to come to its aid. Procedures woven, carpentered, poured, or cantilevered into bioscleave might lead it to nurture life without end, or at least to articulate its lacks and needs, perhaps by delivering them (but does it already do this?) as not-to-be-missed sharp insights.

∞

Adding carefully sequenced sets of architectural procedures
(closely argued ones) to bioscleave will, by making it more
procedurally sufficient, reconfigure supposed inevitability.
                      Closely Argued Built-Discourse Hypothesis

We thus hypothesize that an important recourse available to
those living within an insufficiently procedural bioscleave is to
add procedures back into it. Simply, our species needs to de-
vise and build whatever bioscleave does not spontaneously
provide.

Surely it is plausible to think that if people build into their
surroundings procedures in which to immerse themselves,
bioscleave will grow more procedurally ample. Supplying bioscleave with missing procedures will make it more coherent to
itself and to the members of our species. How shall our species
set about making the bioscleave sufficiently procedural? "Sufficiently procedural for what?" did someone ask? Listen to that
crying. It would be better not only to construct the procedural, but also to have it become one's home ground, one's
training ground. At which point, we trot out our hard-won
notion of an architectural procedure.

Architectural surrounds stage architectural procedures. A
surround constructed to constrain a sequence of actions presents a procedure to be followed; and as soon as someone sets
foot into an architectural surround that constrains action, the
architectural procedure it stages gets going. The constraining
we are speaking of is so light that it is better thought of as
constructive guiding.

Tactically positioned constructed procedures would appear
to be those corrective maneuvers bioscleave has need of to
make it more fully procedural. In a world in which processes

and procedures naturally compound, it is hardly a far reach to think of architectural procedures responding to and expanding on the consequences of other constructed procedures. At such time that the human species will be genuinely able to augment bioscleave, life will have come to be lived on a new basis.

Within tactically posed surroundings (hereafter referred to as tactically posed surrounds) a territory of mediation gets described or suffuses or flourishes in/as place through movements and activities of individuals or groups, or of singles or "withs," as sociologists put it with lovely professional succinctness. Movements and the sited awareness they modulate and that enfolds them mediate architecture; responding to tactically posed surrounds, joining forces with them, actions complete the architectural procedures that put (the) procedural into procedural architecture. Mediating for a person much of what hitherto existed for her as procedural or unconscious, movements and the sited awareness they modulate turn groups of walls and room features, lifeless material, into a more focused, higher level of the procedural. Think of the procedural as having been enlarged to life-size and as now taking place throughout the sited awareness bounded by an architectural surround; the procedural having thus been brought into palpable view, its fixed sequence of actions can be altered. Can it be, then, that in architecture we have the means to construct awareness on a new basis? Oh yes, that is what we have begun to believe.

What Counts as a Closely Argued Built-Discourse?
What Counts as an Architectural Procedure?

It is by relying on juxtaposed repeatable and re-combinable items that verbal discourse, with great sleight of mouth (or hand), encompasses and presents sequentially considered events. Modularly constructed areas and the architectural procedures they engender will be the juxtaposed repeatable and re-combinable items of a built discourse.

An architectural procedure resembles its predecessor, a word, in two respects for a start: first, it is a repeatable item that readily lends itself to discursive use; second, charged with conveying a specific experience or range of experiences, it can be evaluated as to how well it serves its purpose or how effectively it has been put to use.

Architectural procedures used only for studying interactions between body and bioscleave have an observational-heuristic purpose, while those devised for transforming body and bioscleave have a reconfigurative one. Architectural procedures and the tactically posed surrounds that structure and institute them often incorporate both purposes at once, with one purpose grading into another. (See chapter 7 for a more detailed discussion, including descriptions of the first architectural procedures to have come into existence, of what we next allude to only in passing.)

If architectural procedures serve as the words of a built discourse, then tactically posed surrounds, combining these procedures as they do, are its phrases, sentences, paragraphs, and texts. Surely, as well, tactically posed surrounds will factor out as those poems that have ever eluded poets, poems through which those of us who wish to can save our own necks, poems that could only heretofore be intimated by an insufficiently procedural bioscleave. An architectural procedure that helps a person observe more precisely how landing sites disperse may be thought of as an observational-heuristic one, but if, when she performs this procedure, it also provides her with a critical edge on bioscleave, it may be classified as transformational or reconfigurative as well; similarly, if a reconfigurative procedure successfully transforms bioscleave and in the process pinpoints an indistinguishable constituent factor of the person performing it or evinces evidence in support of, for example, the architectural body hypothesis, it serves an observational-heuristic purpose as well. In tactically posed surrounds set up primarily to observe events, houses and towns are constructed as laboratories in which a person's every move can be surveyed, assessed, and reflected upon. Surrounds that run primarily reconfigurative procedures through which to transform biocleave are more training grounds than laboratories. Ideally, tactically posed surrounds should be laboratories that double as training grounds.

If continuity could be maintained across tactically posed surrounds, a built discourse would start up; sequences of tactically posed surrounds would have to be able to be not only consequent on previous sequences but also consequent to ones slated to be built later. Information states produced when someone moves through the slightly different layouts and features of paired tactically posed surrounds would naturally reflect—and inflect and deflect—built-in closely comparable differences; gradations would thrillingly yield a spectrum of body-wide knowing capable of physically manifesting cause and result or warrant and inference.

Not all well-organized enclosures weigh in as the highly structured architectural surrounds we term tactically posed surrounds. Space capsules, for example, despite housing purposefulness aplenty, do not merit the term and therefore do not qualify as works of procedural architecture. An architectural surround that is functional, such as a space capsule, and such as the greater part of the built world of our day, facilitates an organism that persons in its actions, extending the senses no questions asked, whereas an architectural surround that is procedural, a tactically posed surround, fills an organism that persons with questions by enabling it to move within and between its own modes of sensing.

Discursive sequences of tactically posed surrounds, constructed as built propositions, marshal existing logical connectives and position newly invented ones into the "real," steering, regulating, and guiding interactions between body and bioscleave through three-dimensional THEREFORES, BUTS, ORS, ANDS, and built-up WHATEVERS. What will need to be studied is which types and combinations of bodily movements are most conducive to an optimal *tentative constructing toward a holding in place,* and which constructed discursive sequences best constrain them.

A built record of measures taken for remedying bioscleave's insufficiency will rise up with corners and edges, and windows and doors, and hallways and rooms, and streets and crossroads. It will be truly astonishing for someone entering a town to realize that she has set foot within what has been intuited, surmised, and reasoned through, all for the purpose of augmenting her as a member of her species and so that sited awareness (read *architectural body*) can come into its own. Walking along will be discoursing along through an argument of strategic allocations and reallocations. When it stands up to be counted and entered, this built argument or discourse will manifestly turn us inside out, imbuing the ever receptive bioscleave with more of what it is like to be us. We will officially and for all time have put our ruminative selves on view for bioscleave. This will be a depiction in three dimensions (and counting) of how members of our species have fielded what has come to them—what came upon them—as a consequence of their having wielded sited awareness (read *architectural body*) in a coordinated manner. The body moves through a tactically posed town puzzling itself out of focus and then back into it, now with a wider yet sharper focus. Merely by stepping into one's own apartment or that of a friend, one starts the on-the-spot testing of procedural architecture's hypotheses.

A town can be constructed to register the effect a neighboring town has had on the body. This happens to some degree even in nonprocedural towns: Los Angeles has a lot to say to your body about what Chicago or Paris or Singapore has led it to become. But in towns that are closely argued built-discourses, the interchange between body and bioscleave proceeds by means of shaped atmospheric denotations and connotations. One town's assembled constructed statements, its tactically posed surrounds, take up where another's left off, for procedural architecture's subject matter is always the same, with the discussants remaining in all situations body and bioscleave.

Activating an architectural procedure, a person comes alive to her own tacit knowing; body-wide and wider, occurrent tacit knowing goes explicit. A built world, designed with foresight peering through forethought, and that will have been, with great deliberation, arrayed as a communal project, will frame the formation of "the human." In the shadow play of beauty and the beast as one, organism and person, the implicit shines out explicitly. A person stays alive to how she is dispersed and then to how she is again and again dispersed through and into that dispersal. Tacit knowing (knowing how) can then begin to be directly addressed, directly mapped, propositionally, even as propositional knowing (knowing that) can be investigated in regard to how it is bodily—yes, bioscleave, in rapport with you—coordinated to occur.

It arrives to a newcomer moving through town to wonder, "Of the many ways that I could *tentatively construct a holding in place,* which might serve me best in the long run?" The architectural procedures that tactically posed surrounds are set up to run help those enacting them pull together an otherwise all-over-the-map sited awareness. They elicit specific landing-site dispersals, thereby sculpting or molding sited awareness, thereby changing degree of awareness. The subject matter: staying alive/coming alive to/staying alive to. She contrasts in slow motion, or in odd motion, her intricate sitings of herself in terms of this town and the previous one, examining effect and upshot of landing-site dispersal, savvy to the need to identify constituent factors that knit, explode, and weave the world's occurrence. The town has been prepped to recognize and expand on, affirm or negate, in part or in full, what other towns have led her to be able to feel and know. At issue always: what the body can come to know on its own behalf and what the body comes to be able to say to itself.

Because issues of viability are everyone's concern, as are too epistemological conundrums, procedural architecture, a populist architecture of hypothesis, should be approached as a community-wide collaborative initiative. Together the members of our species will exponentially increase the tremendous amount of forethought that is needed for town planning. Exhorted and cajoled by their town, by virtue of being gently constrained by its features and elements, to perform architectural procedures, people work and play at figuring out what in the world they could possibly be. Hypotheses put forward through built form will be predictive of built hypothesizing to come. In a rephrasing of the hypothesis under discussion here, a closely argued built-discourse can foster fundamental reconfigurings of bioscleave that will constitute or lead to a restructuring of viability, to be translated immediately into life on new terms.

It can be argued, of course, that the world has, to some extent, always existed as a built discourse, with people making use of juxtaposed artifacts to address each other. But for a group of constructions—a series of nothing more than inert enclosures, after all—actually "to converse" as a built discourse, systematic conveying will have had to be reasoned through and put in place. An organism that can person is a symbolizing creature that casts thoughts and images upon the faintest anything that gives the slightest indication of being able to in some guise be gotten hold of. Such a creature will easily get traction on and come to think itself through in terms of a world built in a discursive order sequenced to raise existential questions.

A prescriptive supposition, the Closely Argued Built-Discourse Hypothesis presents architecture as the supreme context for the examined life, a stage set for body-wide thought experiments. With architectural procedures prodding the body to know all that it is capable of, this becomes an intrusive and active stage set. The body must either escape or "reenter" habitual patterns of action—habitual actions that have customized life into only a few standard patterns. Upon the body's mastering new patterns of action, biocleave emerges reconfigured.

6
Notes for an Architectural Body

Architectural bodies have everything to do with what a person makes of the fact, the soft but sure-enough fact, that she perceptually subtends, and as-if palpates, architectural surrounds as wholes.

Not a series of actions taken on this scale of action or that but the *coordinating* of several scales of action makes a person able to construct a world. Some scales of action, such as operations that take place in nanoseconds or femtoseconds, are too tiny even to stand up and be counted as scales of action. That which routinely gets coordinated so that a world forms must, even if fleeting, even if immeasurable, continue to be so coordinated, or no actions can be initiated and nothing will form. The coordinating of different scales of action needs to be cut some slack, a great deal of slack—assume it to be the work of all the surroundings and call it an architectural body. Begin by thinking of coordinating one bodily action in conjunction with and in anticipation of another. The coordinating that goes on across a variety of scales of action, a criss-crossing between different world-sizes, continues within and as part of what goes on as basic human-scale bodily coordination. The general phenomenon in muscle control that goes by the name of co-articulation gives a snapshot view of the coordinating of actions or events. A saucer sits on a table at a distance of nearly a foot from its matching cup. A person asked to touch the saucer and pick up the cup at the same time will most likely reach to touch the saucer at the edge nearest the cup while she moves her fingers to be as-if holding the cup's handle even before they reach it. It is through coordinatings such as these that life receives its plausibility. An architectural body might be said to live as a summation of coordinatings of this order.

∞

There is that which prompts (architectural surround) and that which gets prompted (organism-person). Features of the architectural surround prompt the body to act. Actions and maneuvers secure a general taking shape of the surroundings, determining for the body the structure and characteristic features of an architectural surround. In responding to the ubiquitous call that comes from nooks, crannies, and non-nooks and crannies of an architectural surround—most observers feel that they ought eventually to get around to noting everything around them—a person assembles and takes on an architectural body, half-knowingly piecing it together into a flowing whole. The harkening to any feature or element of the architectural surround, bodily stirrings and promptings included: an articulation of the architectural body.

∞

Until a significant number of tactically posed surrounds are in use, the architectural body we hypothesize to exist cannot but make itself scarce. It will be hard to come by except as a heuristic device. Architectural bodies do exist outright in surroundings that are not tactically posed.

∞

An organism casts itself onto the world as a person, and wavers continually between existing as organism and existing as person. Say that all of this casting onto the world and wavering of an organism that persons defines into existence an architectural body.

∞

Above all, an organism-person critically holds in place its assembled "behavings as a person" as a located tentativeness on the move. Architectural body: the dispersing and juxtaposing and culling of landing sites in respect to an architectural surround; a super-convening of many convenings; messenger-like—in rapport with all there is; that which revs as momentum—revved and revving; an amassing of the provisional; a ubiquitous piecing together.

∞

An organism that persons articulates itself and its surroundings through its movements and its landing-site configurations.

∞

Features of the surroundings call forth from organisms-persons the actions and gestures that architect them into persons. On all occasions and any, an organism that persons disperses landing sites, and, by so doing, turns itself into a person having an architectural body.

∞

Through a continual assembling of convened-on sites, an architectural body takes shape near and far. Sectors of the event-fabric interpenetrate in landing embrace, sidling into position. Convened-on sites tremble on the brink as the brink. The world is the brink . . . at the rim. As the architectural body coordinates landing-site activity, sites-on-the-move divide into those that were once landed on and those now being landed on. Incessantly suddenly surfacing or coming around the corner yet once again, penumbral and subliminal landings animate the ubiquitous site of a person within an architectural surround. Ricocheting landings surge up and swoop down, articulating segments of an architectural body. Landing sites land or form not only in the conventional sense of "to land," lowering down to a destination, but also just as often by rising up to one. The sum of all landings convening along the axes of the triad of elemental paired opposites (front-rear, above-below, left-right) that the body continually generates is what formerly went by the name of spacetime.

If organisms form themselves as persons by uptaking the environment, then they involve not only bodies but domains, spheres of activity and influence.

What emanates from bodies and what emanates from architectural surrounds intermix.

A person as a moving body describes an ever-changing sequence of domains, associating herself with some more closely than with others. Surely personing is preferable to person—in the name of accuracy and in the name of tentativeness.

All that emanates from a person as she projects and reads an architectural surround forms an architectural body that moves with her, changing form depending on the positions she assumes. A person's capacity to perform actions is keyed to layout and composition of her architectural body.

∞

Playing to and playing off of that which surrounds it, an organism behaves as a person, and in the process forms now this, now that momentary architectural body.

∞

At its ever-on-the-move edges, the architectural body we hypothesize instantaneously presents itself as shell-like. Within this hint of shell or this enclosing atmosphere that smacks of shell, an organism, pressing against all manner of offered resistance, persons.

∞

If the architectural surround indeed equals nothing more than how it takes shape for the person within it, then the architectural body might be seen as synonymous with it. However, people tend to distinguish between where they are or that within which they are and what they are or what they consider themselves to be subtending.

∞

A summing and rounding up of a person's occurrent landing sites or a grand tour of all a person subtends, the architectural body is of value to us as a heuristic device derived from a heuristic device (landing-site: landing-site configuration).

∞

To be faithful to occurrent tentativeness.

∞

The architectural body is a body that can and cannot be found. Boundaries for an architectural body can only be suggested, never determined.

∞

We speak of an architectural body, rather than an architectural field or an architectural context simply because, to begin with, what we want to describe originates from and joins up with the physical body. Think of the body-proper as lending some of its body to the architectural surround, which, in turn, lends some of what characterizes it as architectural to the body-proper. In addition, the word *body*, used to indicate a collection or quantity of information (as in the expression "a body of evidence"), is descriptively apt for indicating the amassing of landing-site configurations formative of an architectural body. We also find the denoting by the word *body* of a mass of matter that is distinct from other masses (as in the expression "a body of water") useful for conveying all of what belongs to that which we wish to describe, that is, all of what fills an architectural surround, whether that "filling" be counted as "thin air" or "sited awareness."

∞

As well as having to it some of the body of "human body," architectural body has about it some or much of the body of "student body." Have it that "body of sited awareness" parallels not only "body of water" but also "body of work" and "body of thought."

∞

Indeterminate. A mass of indeterminacy. Is there, in fact, an it to this it. Sizeless, or many different sizelessnesses at once. Perspectiveless.

∞

We want to say this body's territory weighs in as a huge ambient kinesthesia, an endowing of the rest of the world with some of the feel of the body-proper's kinesthetic activated (and activating) organismic thickness.

∞

Everywhere one turns: *tentative constructings toward a holding in place;* many *tentative constructings*—and holdings within holdings as latencies and phases—*toward holdings in place.*

∞

Tentative constructings toward holdings in place on many scales of action at once require skillful coordination. An architectural body critically—ever examining and always assessing—holds possibilities in place. The architectural body consists of two *tentative constructings toward a holding in place:* body-proper and architectural surround.

∞

For the purposes of a direct mapping, have symbolic activity or symbolizing—a close relative of imaging capability or derived from it (Construct architectural surrounds through which to investigate this relation!)—be provisionally considered a variety of critical holding. An organism's forming of itself as a person equals its permeating itself with symbolizing. If an organism is knocked off its feet while it is behaving as a person, a person falls; she falls symbolizing, as best she can, herself as a person falling; the landing sites that hold her in place as a person tumble with her, sometimes unable to hold her anymore as a person. Each instant, a person has the ability to handle only a limited amount of critical holding and only a certain amount of symbolizing. The sum of each instant's critical holding: an architectural body.

How to hold onto that which ought not to be allowed to disappear? How to observe and adjust attention's grip on itself? Insert into the world, or into the sequences of landing-site configurations that form it, the edges of a pliable and tentative architecture. Have an architectural surround as the least fragmentary form of sculpture elaborate awareness (landing sites) out into the open. Architecture in the tentative mode can envelop and define a flexible field of knowing.

The drawing out of an organism-person into its personhood is effected within architectural surrounds, which have been fabricated by those whose own personhoods also formed in respect to architectural surrounds.

In cooperation with other organisms, not only synchronically but also in some respects diachronically, the architectural body mediates the body proper and the architectural surround, and it therefore ought to be viewed as communal.

∞

Architectural surrounds have distinct neargrounds, middlegrounds, and fargrounds. Landing-site configurations will articulate at least this many positions: nearnearground, nearmiddleground, nearfarground, middlenearground, middlemiddleground, middlefarground, farnearground, farmiddleground, farfarground; nearmiddlefarground, nearfarmiddleground, middlenearmiddleground, middlenearfarground, farnearmiddleground. But these positions can just as well be thought of as areas of an architectural body, which takes its ubiquitous cue and command from the form and features of an architectural surround, subtending all positions within the surround's confines.

∞

Assigned positions of course quickly lose ground: one moment's nearground slips into the next's farground. Proceduralists insist on taking note of even the most transient of positionings.

∞

In dreams one wields one's body within one's world in an analogous manner to how one positions them in relation to each other in waking life. Think of the famous dream of a woman named Rose who dreamed on the night she succumbed to the deadly 1914 flu of a climbing rose bush clinging to a stone tower only to find upon waking that she, Rose, having fallen victim to paralysis, was clinging for dear life to a stone-like body. In an informal survey of dreams, we found: a hotel in which the dreamer's room cannot easily be returned to because it is on a floor at which the elevators never stop; a hotel elevator that deposits the dreamer on the first floor of a department store at the other end of town or one that shoots right up past the roof into the starry sky; an apartment that is of a distinctly different shape and size from the one the dreamer inhabits in waking life, but in which, she comes to realize, she has been residing for days on end; a narrow, ten-storey high brick tower in which the dreamer is imprisoned, but through whose skylight roof sunlight splendidly pours in; a huge house in Northern Italy to which, a decade ago, the dreamer paid a two-week visit in waking life and in which now, many years later, she, a surprise guest of hosts who are off traveling, plays havoc, in this her recurring dream, with the setting's features and elements even as she fears all the while the imminent return of the missing hosts; rooms that extend the dreamer's waking-life apartment while she sleeps but that with daylight are nowhere to be found. These dreams and countless others should be taken as evidence of how deeply committed to, and intermixed with, its surroundings the body is.

7
Two Architectural Procedures

A person moving through a tactically posed surround will be led to perform procedures that may or may not be recognizable to her as procedures. All of a sudden, what seemed a group of disparate actions, the doing of this and that, may strike her as the steps of a procedure. If these procedures, which have a lot in common with medical procedures, elude their performers, they do so openly, or are constitutionally elusive. Always invented/reinvented on the spot, they exist in the tense of the supremely iffy. Not a fixed set of called-for actions, an architectural procedure is a spatiotemporal collaboration between a moving body and a tactically posed surround.

When tactically posed surrounds corral landing sites, events head for the systematic. Body-wide acquiescing to a procedure buds, then blooms open. Occasionally an enacted architectural procedure will occur as an unquestionably completed sequence of actions, but more often a procedure is engaged in fits and starts; even so, an enacted procedure often has distinct startup, middle course, and endgame momentums. Performing an architectural procedure, a person launches an inquiry-on-the-go into her own constituent factors. As long as that inquiry-on-the-go continues, the procedure has not gone dormant. Just as within the body-proper a good number of bodily processes occur simultaneously, within the architectural body a fair number of procedures can be performed at once.

Architectural procedures disclose, highlight, and explicate the tentative steps by which an organism maintains herself as a person. And so, a sequence of actions (an architectural procedure) eventuates in an investigation into the nature and dynamics of the person performing them. A means for sculpting architectural bodies, an architectural procedure puts organism-person dynamics up for view. Only procedures and proceduralism, not mere form or formalism, can redistribute and reconfigure the architectural body of an organism that persons. It is not to be forgotten that the architectural body, a person's fleeting associating of herself with the whole of what encloses her, fills the whole of the architectural surround, built-in procedures included.

A person trying to reconstruct the circumstances under which a procedure came to take effect must depend on her own memory, but she also receives some help in this effort from the place in which she attempts this feat of memory. It will eventually even become possible for a tactically posed surround to be programmed, for convenience's sake, to prompt someone to recall the tenuous circumstances of a procedure's onset. Beginning to discern what was at stake at the time a procedure blossomed forth, a person—the body—queries her surroundings, "How tentatively did I meet with this procedure and take it on?"

A person who is plunked down in a tactically posed surround, to say nothing of her having simply entered it on foot, immediately asks, "Where am I?" This question has embedded within it an even more direct query, "What am I?" Answers to these questions can only be arrived at through an analysis of the landing-site dispersals of the one seeking an answer. It may be that the two questions will need to be formulated as one: "Where-what am I?" or "What-where am I?" Tactically posed surrounds will be set up to hold open many lines of questioning at once.

∞

Tactically posed surrounds that contrast one segment of world with another prompt sequences of actions that add up to an observational-heuristic procedure we have named the *disperse-to-contrast procedure.* This procedure orchestrates dispersions of landing sites under contrastive conditions that cause them to stand out so as to be more easily assessed. Hypothesizing the upshot of efficient landing-site dispersal to lie in an expanding of capacity to think (to think-feel) and to coordinate actions, we link these two event-fields, coupling landing-site configurations with the expression and behavior with which they appear to coincide. We next contrast different linkages of the two event fields to see if we can specify which landing-site configurations underlie which thoughts and feelings.

Although the constructing of a tactically posed surround that initiates the disperse-to-contrast procedure requires quite a bit more calculating in advance than the putting together of an ordinary house would, actual construction time and costs need not be out of the ordinary. It comes down simply to this—sets of contrastive surfaces and volumes need to be put in place. Two or more instances of a tactically posed surround constructed to be adjacent to one another will yield the desired result, that is, will have effectively produced an enclosed area that will get the disperse-to-contrast procedure going. Architectural surrounds thus paired can be constructed either as identical twins (that they are positioned differently of course precludes identicalness) or as similar volumes containing slight but significant differences. When differences within and between tactically posed surrounds are being compared, the disperse-to-contrast procedure is in progress. Global differences arise when architectural surrounds differ in orientation or scale, or both. Architectural surrounds can be paired as wholes. In our practice we have paired rooms, apartments or houses, areas of terrain (that is, terrain modules), and sections of towns (that is, neighborhood modules). Pairing details of architectural surrounds can produce similar results; that is, duplicating any segment or feature of a room also invites the disperse-to-contrast procedure to spring into action. We have used configurations of walls as modules, repeating them three, four, or five times to generate a wide range of apartments and houses.

Tactically posed surrounds set up to generate or maintain a person's tentativeness in her forming of the world prompt sequences of actions that add up to a reconfigurative or transformational procedure we name the *tentativeness-cradling procedure*. Someone living within a tactically posed surround that houses the tentativeness-cradling procedure will be forever getting her bearings only tentatively. Things take a turn toward the tentative when it is gathered that something basic to all holding in place has been subverted or physically contradicted. A tactically posed surround can be built in which the holding of scale itself, surely basic to all holding in place, doesn't hold. Having once committed oneself, that is, one's landing-site dispersal, to the features of a tactically posed surround in accord with its presented dimensions, one backs away from this commitment, only to find oneself, upon meeting up with expanded or reduced versions of those features, immediately after reasserting this focused commitment, but on a different scale. Everything, each scaled-up or scaled-down feature or object, in comparison with larger or smaller versions of itself, gives one the impression of holding its own but not quite. When scale loses its traction on sited awareness, the tentativeness of the forming moment—raw process, the raw process of venturing forth as existing all up in the air within nearground, middleground, and farground simultaneously— will be seen, heard, and smelled to as-if flutter in the breeze. Taking this further, divide a room into, for example, six sections, each constructed according to a different scale. The tentativeness-cradling procedure cannot help but get underway here. This architectural procedure also blossoms forth within a house of our design that has twenty entrances. Someone having an entrance available to her wherever she turns, with every path she comes upon likely to lead to a welcome mat, will, whether she feels hesitant or not as to where to begin, be continually in the start-again mode, reveling in that tentativeness which the moment just prior to entry brings.

It is no more difficult to set up tactically posed surrounds that produce the sequences of actions that equal in effect the tentativeness-cradling procedure than it is to build surrounds that initiate the disperse-to-contrast procedure. Here are several ways this procedure can be put in place, some of which the above examples have already given some indications of. Construct multiple vantage points in as many ways as possible. For example, build not one but two or more ground planes, giving no preference to one as main, thereby producing double and triple horizons. One can no longer calmly resolve one's view toward a single horizon. Construct more than one scale of operation. Architectural surrounds that reappear in different contexts and thereby generate the disperse-to-contrast procedure will, when repeat occurrences are built at different scales, also harbor the tentativeness-cradling procedure.

The two procedures often get initiated in conjunction with each other, occurring intermixedly. Both procedures are brought to bear as Gulliver moves through Mildendo, the capital of Lilliput. In any event, when we contrast setting foot in tiny Mildendo with traipsing through mammoth London, the disperse-to-contrast procedure is at least verbally invoked. If Mildendo is to survive his visit, Gulliver, who is utterly out of scale for where he is, must move circumspectly and cradle tentativeness in regard to every action lined up in his queue of actions to be initiated (the tentativeness-cradling procedure). It is because the body is capable, if great care is taken, of insinuating itself into a 1:10 scale-model of a metropolis on our scale that Gulliver can succeed in visiting the Lilliputian metropolis Mildendo (not exhibiting the features of London, despite, according to scholars, Swift's firm desire that it be London). A series of scale-models of Mildendo could be generated simply by multiplying or dividing each of the numbers in the passage by the same factor. Gulliver attempts to insert himself into, or simply enters, a metropolis ever again, putting himself through the paces, facing scaled-up or scaled-down objects and features of Mildendo; the reader assesses Gulliver's every move as he proceeds to enter a metropolis that is out of scale for him, guiding decisions about where to place a foot or a hand on a case-by-case, scale-by-scale basis, thereby keeping Gulliver a suitably cautious and considerate interloper.

Taking those numbers that Swift estimates will supply Lilliputians with an ample enough metropolis and multiplying them by a factor of two gives us a 1:5 scale-model of a metropolis on our scale, a new metropolis for tiny organism-persons who are twice the size of Lilliputians (NB: wording of measurements remains Swift's—18th century):

The first request I made after I had obtained my liberty, was, that I might have license to see Mildendo, the metropolis; which the Emperor easily granted me, but with a special charge to do no hurt, either to the inhabitants, or their houses. The people had notice by proclamation of my design to visit the town. The wall which encompassed it is _five foot_ high, and at least _one foot ten inches_ broad, so that a coach and horses may be driven very safely round it; and it is flanked with strong towers at _twenty foot_ distance. I stepped over the great western gate, and passed very gently, and sidelong through the two principal streets, only in my short waistcoat, for fear of damaging the roofs and eaves of the houses with the skirts of my coat. I walked with the utmost circumspection, to avoid treading on any stragglers, that might remain in the streets, although the orders were very strict, that all people should keep in their houses, at their own peril. The garret windows and tops of houses were so crowded with spectators, that I thought in all my travels I had not seen a more populous place. The city is an exact square, each side of the wall being _one thousand foot_ long. The two great streets, which run cross and divide it into four quarters, are _ten foot_ wide. The lanes and alleys, which I could not enter, but only viewed them as I passed, are from _two_ to _three_ feet. The town is capable of holding _five hundred thousand_ souls. The houses are from _three_ to _five_ stories. The shops and markets well provided.

The Emperor's palace is in the center of the city, where the two great streets meet. It is enclosed by a wall of _four foot_ high, and _forty foot_ distant from the building. I had his Majesty's permission to step over this wall; and the space being so wide between that and the palace, I could easily view it on every side. The outward court is a square of _eighty foot_, and includes two other courts: in the inmost are the royal apartments, which I was very desirous to see, but found it extremely difficult; for the great gates, from one square into another, were but _three feet high_, and _one foot two inches_ wide. Now the buildings of the outer court were at least _ten foot_ high, and it was impossible for me to stride over them, without infinite damage to the pile, though the walls were strongly built of hewn stone, and _eight inches_ thick. At the same time the Emperor had a great desire that I should see the magnificence of his palace; but this I was not able to do till three days after, which I spent in cutting down with my knife some of the largest trees in the royal park, about _two hundred yards_ distant from the city. Of these trees I made two stools, each about _six foot_ high, and strong enough to bear my weight. The people having received notice a second time, I went again through the city to the palace, with my two stools in my hands. When I came to the side of the outer court, I stood upon one stool, and took the other in my hand: this I

lifted over the roof, and gently set it down on the space between the first and second court, which was _sixteen foot_
wide.

We leave it to the reader to make all necessary adjustments on
Gulliver's behalf. Multiplying the above set of numbers by a
factor of five brings us to our reality base, the 1:1 scale. After
which, we would find it of particular interest, and of significant procedural architectural moment, to turn right around
and, in small increments, descend from human scale mighty
gradually back down to Lilliputian proportions.

To use the Mildendo passage to generate a work of procedural architecture proceed as follows: Choose an area of the
metropolis on which to concentrate. Put a coherent set of appropriate numbers in the blanks of sentences or paragraphs
describing the area you have chosen. Fill in these blanks several times to produce a group of scale-models, including perhaps even a 1:1 scale-model (ordinarily not thought of as a
model). Erect these scale-models to stand side-by-side.

A person moving from one Mildendo to the other will meet
her own landing-site dispersal along the way, or, at least it
will stand out for her as she moves between scale-models.
Those going back and forth between the Mildendos will feel
themselves to be winds (architectural bodies) blowing into
town, traveling hosts and onrushing landing-site configurations, each time from a different angle and with another scale
of commitment—sentient winds committing to form. Be sure
to have *Directions for Use,* scaled appropriately for each itera-
tion of the urban landscape, on sale in all those parts of town
into which the body (or a hand or foot) can manage to insert
itself.

8
Critical Holder

An implement for examining and assessing what *holds* as what, a critical holder forwards the poetics and the architectonics of cognition and action. It enables a person to discover how she holds the world, that is, it helps her to determine the landing sites with which she holds it, each *holding of the world* equaling a landing-site configuration. This critical apparatus, an add-on to one's own critical apparatus, provides a context in which the body can produce an answer. Training devices that incorporate both the *disperse-to-contrast procedure* and the *tentativeness-cradling procedure,* critical holders put people in contact with their extended bodies, their architectural bodies. How does a person (tentatively) *hold* the world? What holds that which holds a thought? Discerning needs to be noted and examined at those sites at which it lands.

A critical holder is, first and foremost, a construction built to test the Architectural Body Hypothesis/Sited Awareness Hypothesis, which we restate here for the reader's convenience:

> What stems from the body, by way of awareness, should be held
> to be of it. Any site at which a person finds an X to exist should
> be considered a contributing segment of her awareness.

We consider it a great oddity of human life that, even at this late date in history, as straightforward an assertion as this needs to be stated as a hypothesis. This hypothesis points researchers to look at what is at play in and as daily life. If we overflow with a sentient tentativeness (read *awareness*), then transcendence is here and now and can and should be constructively and crisis-ethically continually reworked—the spiritual and the critical become one.

A person who is held in the grip of language alone will have lost touch with many other scales of action vital to her existence.

Stay a moment, says the architectural surround to tentativeness. Tentativeness does hesitate and in so doing provides its landings—that which it lands as—with enough time to form sites. On landing, tentativeness becomes a touch less provisional, a mite less hesitant. That hesitancy within which the landing upon something turns a "corner" on itself and comes to hold forth as or to open up as a site must be judged as simply one of the modes of the tentativeness inherent to body-plus-bioscleave. An area of territory held—a patch or a micro-dot of held territory—can be read as LANDING ACCOMPLISHED AT THIS SITE.

Holding on, whether it is possible to hold on, of course depends on the condition of the one who needs to hold on. What condition a person is in depends on how holding is proceeding on the many different scales of action that both the body and the great, grand, and gentle tentativeness operate on. Tentativeness: feeling and thinking combined.

Day and night, people catch hold of the set of circumstances in their vicinity, only to release that set and go on to attend to the next one to come along.

Critical holders provide their users with an activated and held and holding and activating field set up to coordinate and track landing-site dispersal and to depict and augment a person's coordinating skills. A person accomplishes the swell, cool, meaningful, abrupt, and flowing motions she does, and whatever motions have been left out of this list should be added in, by acquiring and fine-tuning coordinating skills. She holds the architecture that holds her.

Mother held me in her before she held me to her. She held me into (growing me into) my coordinating skills.

The way the body holds itself, the many ways it holds itself, on many different scales of action, and the way it holds the world is cumulative. All the holding you have experienced, all the holding of you and by you, moves within and through your holding of yourself and has a part in your holding onto something.

A baby's first response to its mother's touch is respiratory, and a baby whose mother is attentive learns to breathe effectively that much sooner. Strenuous sucking action is essential for the taking in of nutrients vital to survival, but even so, many babies cannot figure out how to suck until the chin is moved up and down by the mother or a nurse, and a finger, cloth, or pacifier is put into the mouth simultaneously stimulating the upper surface of the tongue and the hard palate to activate the sucking reflex.* As infants learn to coordinate themselves as organisms in a manner sufficient to their needs, development proceeds apace. Becoming increasingly adept at coordinating what needs to be coordinated equals development.

When angry or frustrated, a baby/child/adult will slam closed on—attempt to shut down—some of what it holds itself to exist as: holding its breath; clenching a fist; or withholding anything it can, feces or emotion or . . . —the holding concept.

The *multilevel labyrinth*, a prime example of a critical holder, comes right up close to those within it; it pushes against them

*Margaret A. Ribble, *The Rights of Infants* (Columbia University Press: New York, 1943), 16–17.

or into it they bump should they not have succeeded in grabbing hold of it first.

How convenient that this labyrinth stops the body-proper in its tracks. Within it, people will be able to keep track of near and far components of their architectural bodies. It might be expected that certain combinations of the body's contortings of itself in its attempts to wind past that which blocks its way, as it responds to what it is presented with up-close and what is given to it as distant, will yield a way that more than the usual number of items can be held in mind (read *body*) simultaneously. And so, the linking of the body-proper to an architectural body begins in earnest within the multilevel labyrinth.

Holding its/a/your pattern for you, the multilevel labyrinth looms no less airy and transparent than solid and obscuring. Cutting into formlessness, its layers put a heavy-duty linearity in place for (totally) nonlinear tentativeness to splash out against. Lacking secret passages and with not even a hint of a center, this labyrinth with its many windings and turnings in full view does not need solving; those wishing to puzzle their way out of a labyrinth should not choose this one. Nevertheless, those who enter a multilevel labyrinth will find that it, in true labyrinth spirit, does demand the performing of a difficult but not impossible task. Once within it, one must try to find out how best to use it for an on-site tracing of the architectural body. In the context of a multilevel labyrinth, a path through which one can thread one's way deeply and pervasively and analytically equals an escape route; one escapes into a critical apparatus fitted out for and consequently fit for all dimensions, into a lattice of praxis.

Do not mar tentativeness. One ought not to try and hold onto what one cannot hold onto. How to swim in tentativeness. How to hold tentativeness in (its/your) shape. Do not be greedy: do not

try to hold onto too much. What holds or registers as tentativeness,
that great on-to-the-next . . .

∞

Consider for a moment the critical holder *Gaze Brace,* which
we designed not long before we began work on the multilevel
labyrinth, a few months before it dawned on us how invalu-
able a labyrinth would be for the hunting of the snark which
in our case is the architectural body. At that time, after having
spent several years in some intimacy with a snark named *form-*
ing blank, and having by then started using landing sites heuristically, we reformulated *snark* as *ubiquitous site within a lo-*
cally circumscribed area—or *ubiquitous site,* for short. As the
sum of all occurrent landing sites or the landing-configuration
of each moment, or of each nanosecond, the ubiquitous site
has everything that the architectural body has except X.

We needed a means of showing how changes in bodily position alter the shape of awareness; we realized that any evidence to this effect would be corroborative of the Architectural Body Hypothesis. In the case of ordinary architectural
surrounds, nonprocedural ones, it makes little or no sense to
speak of "the shape of awareness," but when it comes to tactically posed surrounds, this expression is entirely appropriate
and pointedly useful. In any event, we adopt this way of
speaking here for expository purposes only, usually preferring
to speak of what this refers to as a series of landing-site configurations, what a series of landing-site configurations plays
out as, or as the changing contours of an architectural body.

Struck by how greatly a bird's-eye view of a room differs
from a view of it looking straight on, we decided to construct
a room and the bird's-eye view of it side by side. We gave the
constructed bird's-eye view the title *Gaze Brace,* for it was

meant to be a brace for the "shape of awareness." We reasoned that people moving back and forth between a room and its bird's-eye-view twin—the two exactly the same but precisely different—would be able to track with some ease the landing sites they would be obliged to disperse in the course of noticing room features repeated in identical locations, but from radically different vantage points. Objects and features of the ordinary room jut straight out along a steeply inclined floor, in foreshortened form, in the constructed bird's-eye-perspective enclosure. We sought to provide a way for expenditures of energy (by body and by bioscleave) to be logged in so that they could be returned to later and systematically checked up and followed through on.

Taking our lead from vision without wanting to privilege it, we thought, in constructing *Gaze Brace,* of bracing, and making a brace for, or of inventing a steadying apparatus for, of building prosthetic augmentation of some sort for, *all* modes of perception; this way of thinking led us to the multilevel labyrinth.

Who now holds this book has, as our theory goes, an architectural body; but this is an architectural body whose near-ground hogs attention space, letting the rest of the world go hang. When the reading process becomes the coordinating skill that is in ascendancy, when one is engrossed in reading (accord us this), all the following and much else are put on hold: time of day, ambient light, sounds in the vicinity, that one is sitting, and where one is sitting. Everything that asserts its pertinence to something gets put on hold; all that which might be let in or out will be relegated to the background. Hardly any attention can be paid to events that do not forward the main attraction—the reading that continues to read on.

More reading matter: Usually a path is a path and that's that, with this holding true even for paths within mazes. But a path with built-in contradictions, a path that contradicts itself, is another matter, and paths through a multilevel labyrinth do just that. Impulses, impetuses, and movements scatter, and there is no unified trajectory of person to be found when a body is constrained to move in two or more ways at the same time.

The device we will construct together here with you will not do what we say it will do. That is because for the multilevel labyrinth to work it needs to be in physical contact with you and you need to be both guided and blocked by it *as you move through it*. But even so, the device needs to be described or we can't proceed with the discussion.

Let us, then, together as a team, begin to construct here a description of a multilevel labyrinth. Make a loose fist and push it into the book's seam. Choose palm or back of hand and follow the terrain of the 86 pages mounting on the left, then follow the terrain of the pages remaining on the right. That which you are about to construct will help you mete out the world more evenly between nearground and farground, giving every position to come along equal attention space. Once it exists, you will find yourself noting particulars more evenhandedly. The reading process is a coordinating skill, a spate of procedural knowing in active mode that has critical dimensions. But the reading process, which, of course, is a subset of the critical process or the thinking process, removes more critical dimensions than it preserves. A coordinating skill as much as a process, reading can of course have no self-critical dimension; when it tries to read itself it vanishes. Press your fingertips into the book's seam and step out of the reading process and back into the world-at-large once more. All this leads us to a condition of being (read *bioscleave*) that has nothing to say but this: So what?

In the twenty-first century, philosophers need to *construct* the conditions that will cause answers to be forthcoming. To figure out the architectural body, one must literally figure it out into the surroundings. Then let us return to our project of constructing a multilevel labyrinth from scratch. Extricate yourself once again from the reading process to simply stare at the printed page. Count off nine lines including this one, going back up the page or further down it. Forget that. We start again. Take the entire page in evidence. It is the regularity with which this page's lines divide its blank that we want to bring to exist, scaled-up, into the world-at-large. Hold this book (which must be, we easily surmise, opened to this page still) vertically, have it be as vertical as possible. Now expand this page to fit on an 8 × 11 sheet of paper, seeing it as if it were a manuscript page. Breathe through this first expansion now while you still have it. Breathe into its crevices; breathe through and right through the 8-inch-wide blank rows that evince tentativeness because that is what is holding them open. Wedding tentativeness to the provisional is no mean task. But the worded lines on this scale and, indeed, on any scale also live in provisional holding patterns, evincing, too, along with the blanks, a streaming-into-streaming tentativeness; that is, they could never have their (read *their plus your*) say without breathing. Scale the image you are holding up to the height of the tallest tree you can imagine. Difficult? Then let go of that image. Instead, scale the page up to the height of the room that you are in. That's it then. The top line rests on the ceiling and the bottom sits on the floor. The lines extend from one side of the room straight across to the other. The characters spread straight out the back of the virtual sheet of paper (8 × 11) and straight out in front of it as well. But this last bit of the dimensionalizing needed for the description we are striving to assemble jointly might be effected through a different image. You have a hula hoop encircling you, one not needing your gyrations to stay up and around you. Start with a six-inch-thick hula-hoop at hip level. Add enough hula hoops, all at hip level, to glue together a six-inch-thick plane of them throughout the room. Cut into these glued together fifty or so hula hoops to make a labyrinth-layer, bending the hoops to vary the curves and occasionally straightening them to make a more direct path. Make two or three distinctly different labyrinth-layers out of the hula hoop plane. Stacking the labyrinth-layers with one-foot-wide rows of blankness between them, a bit wider proportionately than the blanks accompanying these lines, fill the room with them.

Alternatively, take any labyrinth and shrink it down to six inches high, thinning its walls proportionately. Fit to room size and stack as described above. Insist it a bit further into existence and there you have it—a multilevel labyrinth.

Neither blocking the view nor significantly limiting it, the multilevel labyrinth helps people get a grip on getting hold of taking a hold of the all-over-the-place architectural body. Within it, it will become possible to hold on longer to what would otherwise be, say, merely a fleeting thought as to what that which is over there in the distance might be. It may even become possible to grasp the architectural body in its particulars. Even in this crowd of materials, an atmospheric transparency holds—this is partly the "hold" of "Let's hope the weather holds" and partly that of "Hold onto that rope and then pull yourself along it"—within this structure that makes material note of the many intermediate positions lying between the here's and there's in one's vicinity. A person crossing through a multilevel labyrinth will be engaging perceptually and physically with bars of material segmenting her world. She engages with a bar she finds intriguing because there is something preposterous about it or because she cannot see how it fits into the labyrinth-layer it would seem to belong to; she heads in one direction, only to find a number of bars that would certainly seem to be guiding her in several other directions. Hence we refer to rods of material assembled into the cutout patterns of the labyrinth-layers as both guiding and engaging bars. What if, when passing around, with some difficultly, a curve (a four-foot-long, forty-degree segment of a circle with a ten-foot radius) expressed in RUBBER, you were to catch a glimpse of the same curve in STONE or, say, in FUR. Because, at the same time the curve rests against you, a rubbery, constant, gentle pressing curving around your hips, you hold a view of it in two other textures as well, you find yourself catching a glimpse not only of texture and shape but, in effect, of the dynamics of *holding textures and shapes in view.*

This labyrinth-layer is RUBBER/STONE/FUR. *Do you see and touch this as* RUBBER/STONE/FUR? *I hold it as* RUBBER/STONE/ FUR. RUBBER/STONE/FUR *to me. I too hold it to be* RUBBER/ STONE/FUR. RUBBER/STONE/FUR *it communally is for us then— in language—in world—in landing sites.*

Bodily inserting every last finger of herself into the multilevel labyrinth, she propels and squeezes her body through it; around she curls past what bars the way, bodily threading through this demanding—and yet, on its own terms, accommodating—labyrinth. The body angles itself through and over, moving at several angles to itself at once, neck curving around an obstacle, head part of a different curve, midsection pulled in, one leg striding forward and the other positioned with a bent knee, its calf and thigh pressing into each other. One shoulder bends toward the chest, the other juts out in back; she elbows and shoulders and elbows, and pushes and pulls, and otherwise insinuates bone and flesh to gain, ever again, traction so as to inch and cram, wedge, and, in full flesh, secrete herself through a lattice that by impinging on her trajectory as a person gives her the many trajectories of an architectural body.

An organism-person likes there to be one world, for this makes it easier to be one person at a time. And there is no doubt that it is useful to be one person at a time. But the question is, is it useful enough?

What a subsuming entity a person turns out to be. Mostly, divergent impulses and initiatives get reported in typically reduced fashion as simply how a person feels at the moment.

It would be best, when studying how one is apportioned out, to remain aware of a bipartite nearground nestling within a bipartite middleground nestling within a bipartite farground. Each of these regions could be further divided, with a bipartite nearground, for example, presented as encompassing a bipartite nearnearground, middlenearground, and farnearground.

In any event, because it is where the front-nearground and the back-nearground meet, the home base of the body ought to be thought of as the nearnearground. Not until tactically posed surrounds have been set up for investigating where to draw the line between the body-proper and the architectural body will it be possible to determine whether or not the body-proper's domain reaches out beyond the nearnearground to subtend the bipartite middlenearground as well. In any event, we refer to the body as the nearnear because, to the organism-person whose body it is, nothing is nearer or more foregrounded or more foreforegrounded. But when it comes to delineating positionings for the body-proper, lighthearted foregrounding will, of course, not be sufficient. The historical record and contemporary existence alike reveal the matter of positioning in relation to a body in action to have hardly been broached at all. Although the body-proper is thick or rife with its own sets of landing sites, it does not allow for—it would appear not to be roomy enough for—there to be any stepping back far enough within it for there to be a peering into some distant farground of the nearnear; but with a change in scale of operation and a playing of one scale of operation off another even this might become possible. Speaking of a nearearground slightly increases the body-proper's domain, giving it a bit more volume within and through which to negotiate its path.

The sum of what (of bioscleave) the nearnear lends itself to guides it in its moving and speaking. A person, a critical holder in her own right, but one in need of assistance, upon giving herself over to (read *lending her all to*) that critical holder known as the multilevel labyrinth, begins an exegesis of the nearnear and the farfar and everything in between; critiquing her surroundings, she expands on both the rationally and the irrationally "closed down" so as to be able to figure out urgent matters of crisis-ethical import; interpreting and exposing within and between automatisms as she goes, she examines how many scales of action she is in need of for holding herself in place or for holding herself to a path or for holding an image or a thought; analyzing out into the open her own explanatory power, she explicates with a newfound thoroughness both degree of willingness and degree of tentativeness; and, upon having reconstrued and reconfigured construal itself, she proceeds to bring many scales of action to bear at once.

You will be able to return to an image or thought you want to return to, if you don't tense up on it, and if you don't hold yourself too tightly or too differently from the way you were holding yourself when it first surfaced as an image or when you first thought of it; if you keep the tentativeness flowing and shaping out, it will come back.

Reined in by a labyrinth's narrow passageways, the architectural body stays near and tactility comes immediately into play. The architectural body can receive its first-ever checkup. Together visual, aural, tactile, kinesthetic, and olfactory landing sites delineate front-nearground, front-middleground, and front-farground and back-nearground, back-middleground, and back-farground. The architectural body is able to receive its checkup because at last a "body" otherwise suspended in thin air has begun to land as a body; the architectural body hangs itself out to live on the multilevel labyrinth. Another way to put this is that a major part of the architectural body need no longer be merely imaged as such, for occasions for perceptual landings proffered by this new type of labyrinth cause the body-proper's tentatively extending and extended (world-endowing; world-imbuing; world-declaring) body to become more palpable.

On a bright and sunny day, you are out for a stroll through an urban landscape, a modular town if ever there was one, a town to give new meaning to modularity. You live in this town and you are out for a walk in it. When strolling through your neighborhood, through Module L, for example, suddenly, upon rounding the third of the seven bends of a long, winding lane, you find yourself wondering, "What would it feel like to walk this same winding path in Module J?" You get yourself over there. A bit out of breath, having raced over to the "same spot" at breakneck speed, you figure out, bodily, how to reassume the mantle of yourself, striving to hold your body as you did during the initial phase of this stroll. The internal (body-wide) command might be: As you were.

Having positioned yourself as you were positioned prior to the urge to experiment, you pick up the stroll where you had left off, surrounded, as you go, by each of the landmarks peculiar to this lane, alike in all respects to the ones that would have surrounded you had you stayed on your own turf (Module L, home base). At first, not that different, how your body feels here as opposed to there. No, that's not true.

Even if Modules J and L, the two producers of and contexts for the country lane upon which you stroll, had identical orientations and terrain contours, which they don't, a held (and holding) image of your wending foray along precisely this path during the initial phase, when you were in Module L, would pervade your strolling further along upon it in Module J. Your strolling along within Module J would similarly not be held neutrally apart from thoughts and images as to what might have transpired at the same spot had you held to the path in Module L. Simply more of the same? Oh yes, very much so, and, oh no, not really. Visiting imaging landing sites upon occurrent perceptual landing sites, the doubling of a coordinating skill such as walking or strolling will inevitably lead to a person's finding her body to be an architectural body. Giving further amplitude and heft to a nearnear, the kinesthetic mode would be operating at its suffusing best, cascading through the body and structuring it to be ripe for a brand-new, wider-than-ever hold on itself. Kinesthetically "whispered" or "Kinesthetically" whispered: "Here could have been [is!] there (and vice versa) and still could be!"

9
Daily Research

Revisiting the three hypotheses of procedural architecture, we get the following: A person and her surroundings need to be weighed in together as an architectural body, or, put more directly, the inextricability of person and bioscleave must at all costs be respected. The totally mad and relentless wasting away of life—bodies-proper and their extended or architectural bodies alike—is a consequence of a fundamental procedural insufficiency of bioscleave; that is, bioscleave, if looked at from the perspective of those who want to live and are even so routinely denied life, should be taken as being, although magnificently great, half-baked (read *insufficiently procedural*). But in this we have a condition that may, at least on a local level and on a case-by-case basis, be reparable.

A crisis ethicist, by definition a person who judges all ethical systems not unconditionally supportive of life to be bankrupt, and who, not leaving a stone unturned, be it a pebble or a planet, be it a cardboard stage prop or a stony nanospeck, endeavors to reverse the abhorrent human condition, will be led by the logic of the argument that the three hypotheses of procedural architecture present to turn herself into an architect, a procedural architect. Here are these hypotheses once again together with design principles that follow from them.

> What stems from the body, by way of awareness, should be held
> to be of it. Any site at which a person deems an X to exist should
> be considered a contributing segment of her awareness.
> Architectural Body Hypothesis/Sited Awareness Hypothesis

• Tactically posed surrounds should be designed for the purpose of making landing-site dispersal (disposition/placement of sited awareness) readily noticeable.
• Tactically posed surrounds should be designed for the purpose of altering the proportions in which different types of landing sites are dispersed.

It is because we are creatures of an insufficiently procedural
bioscleave that the human lot remains untenable.
                    Insufficiently Procedural Bioscleave Hypothesis

• An important purpose of tactically posed surrounds is the adding of procedures (for the body) to the insufficiently procedural (for the body) bioscleave.

Adding carefully sequenced sets of architectural procedures
(closely argued ones) to bioscleave will, by making it more
procedurally sufficient, reconfigure supposed inevitability.
                    Closely Argued Built-Discourse Hypothesis

• Contiguous tactically posed surrounds should be close variations (closely argued) on each other for that will allow the body to keep track of the effect architectural procedures have on it.

How the body gets, how it disperses, and how it replenishes its energy—these are all questions with enormous crisis-ethical import. Conditions and situations most beneficial to the body will be those that deplete it the least and that most swiftly replenishes it.

∞

A Crisis Ethicist's *Directions for Use*
(Or How to Be at Home in a Residence-Cum-Laboratory)

1. Play off of your tactically posed surround like crazy until you have constructed a precise tentativeness for yourself.

2. Vary the size and shape of your body by dwelling into your linkings-up with features and elements of your tactically posed surround. (Further explanation: Any linking up with a feature or element equals one landing site or many.)

3. Attempt to assign more than one size and shape at a time to the body you take to be yours for the nonce.

4. To surpass automaticity—organism-person automaticity —re-route landing-site dispersal. (Further explanation: Think in terms of holding the world in a vise of landing sites that can be relaxed.)

5. Seek out the many scales of action on which landing— the sterling event of coming to land—occurs within the body that you take to be yours for the nonce.

6. Strive to maintain your extended body as more than a single subsuming tentativeness; that is, cast your landing sites out and about to form several extended domains of indeterminacy. (Further explanation: An architectural body expresses and materializes through a relentless drive [on the part of an organism-person] to disperse as landing-site configurations. Maintaining an architectural body requires the continual stirring up of plausible indeterminacy.)

7. Make an effort to catch those moments at which procedure (architectural procedure) joins up with/overtakes/ supplants process (biophysical, physiological, metabolic, psychological processes).

8. When attempting to note the degree to which you are communal, register any scale of action that you are at all cognizant of as a constituting member of the community which is you. (Further explanation: Formed in good measure of dis-

parate groups of elements and features encountered, an organism that persons lives as a community.)

9. While attending to your front farnearground, for example, or your front nearfarground, for that matter, try lingering as well within and upon the nearnear and the farfar. (Further explanation: What permutations of sited awareness best sketch into existence non-collapsing lucidity?)

10. Use slight differences between areas of your tactically posed surround to estimate proportionate contribution of each type of landing site to the perceptual array that holds waveringly in place as a world for you.

11. In two or more nearly identical areas within your tactically posed surround, contrast the landing sites—approximately how many and roughly in which locations—that suffice for the tentativeness of each moment to be held waveringly in place as a world for you.

12. Associate your bodily actions so strongly with your tactically posed surround that they become as if integral to it. (Further explanation: Embracing and cradling the tentativeness that precedes and accompanies action and sympathizing with and emulating the mutability inherent to a moving body, your tactically posed surround, set up to be reaching out to you femtoseconds before you find yourself reaching out to it, invites you to be, in advance of any overture from you, ever and again part of it.)

13. Ally yourself that closely with your tactically posed surround that it reads as the perimeter of your extended body. (Further explanation: Your body complies with presented structures through landing-site dispersals that are determinative of its [body-proper's/architectural body's] holding patterns. Not only an eventuality for your consideration, this desired integration, if seen from the perspective of the Architectural Body Hypothesis, will be recognized as already having taken place.)

14. Attempt a massive unholding. Have your tactically posed surround's hold on you loosen even as you loosen your hold on it.

15. To press the restart button, to start afresh, becoming as if an infant—suffusing your as-if adult with an as-if infant— find what is tentative within and throughout what declares itself as definitely in place.

16. Observe how your body adjusts to enclosures of different sizes, taking note of how its density and expanse change depending on the size of the area in which it is enclosed and on how it lands on and holds onto surrounding elements and features.

17. Avail yourself of your tactically posed surround to disperse your landing sites of the moment in such a way as to prevent the coming into existence of a world for you.

18. Observe whether tactically posed surrounds devised to lighten your imaging load actually do; that is, see if they reduce the number of imaging landing sites (by increasing the number of perceptual landing sites) needed to hold tentativeness waveringly in place as a world for you.

19. To determine the degree to which imaging load (number of imaging landing sites necessary to hold the world in place for you) influences coordinating ability, run tests of memory and skill in areas set up to lighten imaging load. Test results from these areas should outshine those from areas demanding extensive imaging-landing-site dispersal.

20. Have it that it is always a matter of sculpting your sited awareness and comparing resulting sculptures (architectural bodies). Room A is an upside-down version of Room B. Assuming that you perform the same set of movements in each room, it might then be expected that your architectural body assembled in respect to room A will be the same as room B's only inverted.

21. Dip at will into, so as to further reflect on, the free-ranging

would-be connectivity out of which cohesiveness for architectural bodies is fashioned; sporadically play a cleaving (cutting apart from while adhering to) hesitation waltz with tendencies, inclined breezes and pursuits, and rivulets of complexly varied sited awareness. Will some joining-in or joining-together areas blast back to you the schematics of their conjugated articulating snap-to's?

TO BE CONTINUED . . .

To what else life will be able to originate as because of what architecture will have become

About the Authors

For the last forty years, artists-architects-poets Madeline Gins and Arakawa have created a visionary and widely admired body of work—museum installations, landscape and park commissions, experimental texts and films, residential and office designs, philosophical treatises and artistic manifestos—that challenge traditional notions about our built environments and the ways we inhabit them. Their transformations of physical space have consistently explored the poetics of architecture and the nature of contemporary life and thought.

Since 1981, with the inception of their theory of *reversible destiny*—the belief that through radical forms of architecture mortality itself can be undone—they have dedicated themselves to rethinking the relationships between architectural environments and the body.

In 1997 the Guggenheim Museum presented a retrospective of Arakawa and Gins's collaborative work, which received the College Art Association's highest award for that year (the Artist Award for Exhibition of the Year: Distinguished Body of Work, Presentation or Performance Award), and published a widely acclaimed catalogue of their work titled *Reversible Destiny: WeDestiny (We Have Decided Not to Die)*. Additionally, their work has been the subject of many critical studies by, among others, Jean-François Lyotard, Arthur Danto, Italo Calvino, George Lakoff, and Hans-Georg Gadamer. Their more recent projects include "Nagi's Ryanji," a thirty-foot-diameter tube having both left-right and above-below symmetry, and "The Site of Reversible Destiny," a seven-acre park. Currently, two projects based on the design principles outlined in the present text are under way: construction has begun on Bioscleave House, a private dwelling commissioned by a family in East Hampton, New York, and schematic drawings have been completed and delivered for Reversible Destiny Eco-Housing Park—a reversible destiny community of several hundred units.

Books by Arakawa and Gins

Mechanismus der Bedeutung (The Mechanism of Meaning). Trans. Carlo Huber. 1st ed. Munich: Bruckmann, 1971. Introduction by Lawrence Alloway.

For Example (A Critique of Never). Trans. Aldo Tagliaferri. Milan: Alessandra Castelli, 1974.

The Mechanism of Meaning, 2nd ed. New York: Harry N. Abrams, 1979. Published in French as *Le Mécanisme du sens.* Trans. Serge Gavronsky. Paris: Maeght Editeur, 1979. Trans. Shuzo Takiguchi and Kiichiro Hayashi. Published in Japanese as exhibition catalog. Osaka: National Museum of Art, 1979.

Pour ne pas mourir/To Not to Die. Trans. François Rosso. Paris: Editions de la Difference, 1987. Published in Japanese. Trans. Masashi Miura. Tokyo: Libroport, 1988.

The Mechanism of Meaning, 3rd ed. New York: Abbeville, 1988. Published in Japanese in two volumes. Tokyo: Seibu Museum of Art and Libroport, 1988.

ARCHITECTURE: Sites of Reversible Destiny (Architectural Experiments after Auschwitz-Hiroshima.) London: Academy Editions, 1994.

Reversible Destiny. New York: Guggenheim Museum/Abrams, Inc., 1997.

Books by Madeline Gins

Word Rain or A Discursive Introduction to the Intimate Philosophical Investigations of G,R,E,T,A G,A,R,B,O, It Says. New York: Grossman, 1969.

Intend. Bologna: Tau/ma, 1973.

What the President Will Say and Do!! Barrytown, NY: Station Hill, 1984.

Helen Keller or Arakawa. Santa Fe: Burning Books; New York: East-West Cultural Studies, 1994.